A PICTURE TREASURY
of Good Cooking
A TESTED RECIPE INSTITUTE COOK BOOK

BY

DEMETRIA M. TAYLOR
Home Economics Director

AND

LILLIAN C. ZIEGFELD
Executive Home Economist

photographs by
ALBERT GOMMI

BOOKS WRITTEN BY DEMETRIA M. TAYLOR

CAESAR SALAD.
page 62

A PICTURE TREASURY
of Good Cooking

Table of Contents

A PICTURE TREASURY *of Good Cooking*

This book brings you superb recipes with good-cooking-appeal, and 104 full-color pictures with appetite-appeal to make an adventure not only of eating but of cooking too.

The lavish use of pictures is the result of a long study made by Tested Recipe Institute which shows that pictures in color are what you, today's cook, want in your cookbook. We feel that by making cooking more glamorous and interesting for you, this book will make cooking and serving meals to your family an easy and enjoyable part of your daily life. By showing in the picture not only the major dish but also accompanying dishes you can pick up menu ideas for appetizing, well-balanced meals.

These recipes were created by Miss Taylor, our Home Economics Director, for the beginner as well as the experienced cook. She has simplified them, and removed guesswork to assure success to your cooking. Each recipe has been tested for taste perfection in the kitchens of the Tested Recipe Institute. The directions are clear and easy-to-read; the ingredients are carefully described; the time and temperature for baking and cooking are included and the number of servings is noted. There are sections with buying ideas to help you with your marketing.

Included are several pages of complete menus and a section with suggestions for using leftovers that will make the second meals from your roasts anticipated events for your family. There are also variations that add "spice" to many basic recipes.

Annette Rhys has done a grand job of food styling and preparation for the book and Ernestine Stowell spent countless hours hunting for the accessories and planning the table settings for the pictures.

As you use these recipes, we at Tested Recipe Institute feel that A PICTURE TREASURY OF GOOD COOKING will soon come to be a familiar and dependable friend in your kitchen.

ROBERT L. LEWIN, President
Tested Recipe Institute, Inc.

ONION SOUP

2 tablespoons butter or margarine	4 cups hot water
1 teaspoon sugar	2 tablespoons meat-extract paste or 6 beef-bouillon cubes
1/4 teaspoon dry mustard	4 slices buttered French bread
2 cups sliced onion	1/4 cup grated Parmesan cheese

Melt butter in a large saucepan; blend in sugar and mustard. Add onion; cook over low heat, stirring frequently, about 15 minutes, or until tender but not brown. Pour in water; bring to boiling. Blend in and dissolve meat extract (for a rich dark soup) or bouillon cubes (for a light, delicately-flavored soup). Simmer, uncovered, about 15 minutes. Pour into individual heat-proof serving bowls. Top with slices of bread; sprinkle with cheese. Broil, 3 inches from heat, 2 to 3 minutes, or until cheese is golden-brown. Makes 4 servings.

PUREE MONGOLE: Combine **1 can each pea soup and tomato soup**; blend in equal amount of **milk**; heat to serving temperature.

SCOTCH SOUP: Combine 1 can **Scotch broth** and 1 can **bean with bacon soup**. Gradually blend in an equal amount of **water**; heat slowly to serving temperature.

5

HEARTY BEEF AND VEGETABLE SOUP

1 pound lean stewing beef, cut in
   1-inch pieces (chuck, shin, neck)
1 beef knucklebone, cracked
6 cups water
1 No. 2 can (2½ cups) tomatoes
2 cups diced potatoes (2 large)
2 cups diced carrots (6 medium)
1 cup diced celery (2 large stalks)

1/2 cup chopped onion
   (1 medium)
1/4 cup pearl barley
6 whole cloves
1 bay leaf
1 tablespoon salt
1 teaspoon sugar
1/8 teaspoon pepper

1 cup diced white turnips (2 small)

Place all ingredients in deep kettle; cover. Turn heat high; heat soup mixture to boiling. Turn heat low; simmer 1½ to 2 hours, or until meat is tender; remove bones. Chill overnight. Skim off fat. Reheat. Serve piping hot. Makes about 4 quarts.

SOUP CUES: Any soup with a broth or milk base that is to be stored must be cooled **quickly** before it is placed in the refrigerator. (Slow cooling allows harmful bacteria to multiply). Set the kettle in cold water, and keep changing the water as it warms.

Try your hand at combining two or more varieties of canned soup. You will be delighted with the new flavors you create.

OYSTER STEW

1/4 cup butter or margarine	1 quart raw oysters*
1 teaspoon Worcestershire	1½ quarts milk
Dash paprika	1½ teaspoons salt

Dash pepper

Melt butter in deep pan. Add Worcestershire and paprika; stir until smooth. Add oysters and oyster liquor; cook over low heat until edges of oysters curl. Add milk, salt, and pepper; heat thoroughly over low heat but do not boil. Makes 6 servings.
*Or 2 packages quick-frozen oysters.

CREAM OF OYSTER SOUP

Strain liquor from **1 pint oysters**; reserve. Chop oysters fine. Add to liquor with **1 tablespoon minced onion** and **1 small bay leaf.** Simmer 10 minutes; remove bay leaf. Add oyster mixture to **3 cups thin white sauce***; cook over hot water 15 minutes, stirring occasionally. Just before serving, add **1 tablespoon minced parsley.** Garnish each serving with **paprika.** Makes 6 servings.
***3 tablespoons each butter and flour, 3 cups milk, salt,** and **pepper.**

CREAM OF CARROT SOUP

3 tablespoons butter or margarine	3 cups milk
1 tablespoon chopped onion	3 cups shredded carrots
3 tablespoons flour	2/3 cup boiling salted water
1 teaspoon salt	1/3 cup light cream
Dash pepper	Paprika, chopped parsley

Melt butter in large saucepan. Add onion; cook till soft. Blend in flour, salt, and pepper. Add milk; cook till thickened, stirring constantly. Cook carrots in water 10 minutes; add to milk mixture. Just before serving, add cream. Garnish with paprika and chopped parsley. Makes 6 servings.

CREAM OF VEGETABLE SOUP

Proceed as for Cream of Carrot Soup. Instead of cooked shredded carrots and water, add **2 cups sieved cooked vegetable,** such as broccoli, peas, lima beans, or any desired mixture of leftover, cooked vegetables, sieved. If a strong flavored vegetable is used, the onion may be omitted.

SPLIT PEA SOUP

1 cup dried green split peas	1½ quarts water
Beef knuckle, cracked or ham bone	1 bay leaf
1 No. 2 can (2½ cups) tomatoes	1 teaspoon salt
1 medium onion, peeled and chopped	Dash pepper

Wash and pick over peas. Add remaining ingredients. Cover; simmer 2 hours, stirring occasionally. If the soup thickens too much, add additional boiling water. Remove bone. Press soup through sieve. Serve hot with croutons. Makes 6 servings.

BLACK BEAN SOUP

Cover **2 cups black beans** with **cold water;** soak overnight. Drain; measure liquid. Add **water** to make 2 quarts; pour into kettle. Add beans, **1 large onion, sliced, 1/2 cup diced celery, 1 teaspoon salt, 4 peppercorns.** Cover; simmer 3 hours, or till beans are tender; add **water** if necessary. Put through food mill or sieve. Add **1/4 teaspoon dry mustard.** Blend **3 tablespoons butter or margarine** and 1½ **tablespoons flour;** stir into soup slowly. Heat thoroughly. Garnish with **lemon slices.** Makes 6 servings.

CREME VICHYSOISSE

4 leeks	1 cup light cream
3 cups sliced pared potatoes	1 cup milk
3 cups boiling water	1 teaspoon salt
4 chicken bouillon cubes	1/4 teaspoon pepper
3 tablespoons butter or margarine	2 tablespoons minced chives
1/4 teaspoon paprika	

Cut leeks with 3 inches of green tops into fine pieces. Cook leeks and potatoes in water, covered, until tender, about 40 minutes. Press, without draining, through a fine sieve into top of double boiler. Add next 6 ingredients; stir well. Heat over hot water. Serve hot or thoroughly chilled, garnished with chives and paprika. Makes 6 servings.

OKLAHOMA BISQUE

Combine in a large saucepan **two 10½- or 11-ounce cans condensed tomato soup, 2 cups milk, 1/8 teaspoon onion salt, dash pepper,** and a **12-ounce can whole kernel corn.** Heat slowly to serving temperature; do not allow to boil. Add **3 tablespoons butter or margarine.** Makes 6 servings.

Meats are the Mainstay

If you ask the man of the house what he'd like for dinner, chances are he'll name the meat, and leave the rest of the menu up to you. For, in his opinion, the meat makes the meal!

HOW TO BUY MEAT

Quality influences price. You have to be an expert to judge quality by eye alone. It's safer to depend on a packer's brand or a government grade. Meat packers stamp their own brand on better quality meats, with the exception of pork. Fresh pork is seldom branded because its tenderness does not vary as much as other meats. Government grades are no longer compulsory, but some packers still request such grading—"U.S.D.A. Prime," "U.S.D.A. Choice," and "U.S.D.A. Good" are grades found on retail cuts.

All meats that are shipped in interstate commerce are subject to federal inspection and are stamped with a round, purple insignia which assures the buyer that the meat is wholesome. You will find this same legend on packaged meats.

Seasons influence cost, and when a meat like lamb is out of season and expensive, another meat will be in season and less expensive.

Of course supply and demand influence meat prices, also. For example, if you live in a round-steak neighborhood you may find that porterhouse or T-bone steak is a real bargain, because it is not in demand.

Shopping for meat is much easier than it used to be. The meat departments in supermarkets feature displays of meats, already weighed, wrapped in transparent paper, and plainly marked as to price. This is a great help to inexperienced shoppers, women with small families, and business women who do not have time to wait while meat is selected, cut, weighed, and wrapped.

Your kitchen shelf should certainly hold a supply of several of the many excellent canned meats that are available—luncheon meat, corned beef hash, chili con carne, potted meats and pastes, or spreads, Vienna sausages, frankfurters, hamburgers, and whole ham, to name the most popular kinds. They will prove to be life-savers, time and time again when emergencies arise.

If you have a home freezer, or a large frozen storage compartment in your refrigerator, be sure to keep some packaged quick-frozen meats on hand—small steaks, chops, a small roast, hamburger, and so on to fall back on some rainy evening or for unexpected guests.

We have had difficulty selecting the recipes that follow, picking and choosing from our favorites. All we can say is—these are tops!

ROAST BEEF

STANDING RIB ROAST (picture below): Select a roast, allowing 1/3 to 1/2 pound of meat per person. For best results, roast at least 2 ribs.
ROLLED RIB ROAST (see picture, back cover): Select a 6- to 8-pound roast, boned and rolled.

You must know the weight of the roast to estimate cooking time. Have the meatman weigh meat after trimming or weigh it at home.

Wipe meat with a damp cloth. Season with salt and pepper, if desired. Place in an open roaster or baking pan. (Place standing roast, fat side up, a rolled roast on a rack.) Roast in a moderately low oven, 325°F., using table below. Do not cover, add water, or baste.

Use a meat thermometer to insure best results. Insert bulb so it rests in thickest part of meat without touching fat or bone. Thermometer should read 140° F. for rare, 160° F. for medium, 170° F. for well-done, regardless of weight or type of roast.

ROAST BEEF TIMETABLE

If roast weighs:	And you like your meat:	Approximate minutes per pound for Standing Rib:	Boned and Rolled:
3 to 5 pounds	Rare:	26	
	Medium:	30	
	Well-done:	35	
6 to 8 pounds	Rare	20	30
	Medium:	25	35
	Well-done:	30	40

Recipe for French Fried Potato Puffs (around roast), page 13

LONDON BROIL

1 top quality flank steak,　　**1 3-ounce can broiled sliced**
　2 to 2½ pounds　　　　　**mushrooms**
　　　　　　　　1 can beef gravy

Place flank steak on broiler rack in preheated broiler 3 inches from heat. Broil 4 to 5 minutes on each side. Slice diagonally in thin slices across grain of the meat. Add mushrooms, liquor and all to gravy; heat; pour some of the gravy over the beef slices; serve the remainder separately. Makes 6 servings.

FRENCH FRIED POTATO PUFFS
(see picture at left)

Combine **2 cups leftover, seasoned mashed potatoes, 2 well-beaten eggs,** and **4 slices crumbled, crisp bacon.** Sift together **1 cup sifted flour, 2 teaspoons baking powder,** and **1 teaspoon salt.** Stir into potato mixture. Blend well. Heat fat, 2 inches deep, in a deep fat fryer or a deep pan to 375°F. on a fat thermometer, or until a 1-inch cube of bread browns in about 40 seconds. Drop potato mixture by spoonfuls into fat. Fry 3 to 5 minutes, or till brown. Excellent with Roast Beef. Makes 6 servings.

13

BROILED STEAK

Beef cuts suitable for broiling are porterhouse or T-bone, rib steak, club steak, sirloin, or rump from good quality beef. Steaks may vary from 1 inch to 2 inches in thickness.

Preheat broiler. Wipe meat with a damp cloth and cut fat on edges. Place on broiler rack with surface of meat 3 to 3½ inches from heat. Broil for half the time required. See Timetable below. Season cooked side with salt and pepper; turn, and finish broiling. Stick fork into fat to turn.

Broiling time depends not on weight but on thickness of steak. Steak is best when cooked rare or medium. The fine flavor is lost if it is cooked well-done. Broiled steak should be attractively browned, with juicy interior of the desired doneness.

Steak may be pan-broiled. Heat a little suet or fat in a skillet; cook steak for half the time required in the timetable.

TIMETABLE FOR BROILING STEAK

For Steaks:	Broiling time (approximate) for rare:	Broiling time (approximate) for medium:
1 inch thick	8 to 10 minutes	12 to 14 minutes
1½ inches thick	14 to 16 minutes	18 to 20 minutes
2 inches thick	20 to 25 minutes	35 to 40 minutes

ROLLED STUFFED FLANK STEAK

2 tablespoons butter or margarine	Dash pepper 3 tablespoons hot water
1 medium onion, chopped	1 egg, well- beaten
3 cups soft bread crumbs	1 flank steak (about 2 pounds)
1/2 teaspoon poultry seasoning	2 tablespoons fat or salad oil
1/2 teaspoon salt	1/2 cup boiling water

Melt butter in a large skillet. Add onion. Cook until golden brown. Add next 6 ingredients and mix well. Spread on steak. Roll up like a jelly roll; tie securely with string. Heat fat in the skillet. Brown meat on all sides. Sprinkle with additional salt and pepper; add water. Cover; bake in moderately low oven, 325°F., 1½ hours, or until meat is tender. Makes 6 to 8 servings.

BEEF STROGANOFF: Peel **3 pounds onions.** Put through a food chopper, using coarse blade. Drain. Save juice. Heat **1/3 cup fat** in a large, heavy saucepot. Add onions; cook over low heat 20 minutes. Add **2 pounds top round steak,** sliced very thin, and **1 pound mushrooms,** sliced. Cook until brown. Add reserved onion juice, **a 6-ounce can tomato paste,** a **10½- or 11-ounce can condensed tomato soup, 1 cup sour cream, 1 teaspoon salt, 1/8 teaspoon pepper, 1 teaspoon Worcestershire.** Stir well. Cover; simmer 1 hour, stirring occasionally. Makes 6 servings.

DE LUXE MEAT LOAF

1 egg, beaten	2 cups soft bread crumbs
3/4 cup milk	1 onion, minced
1 teaspoon poultry seasoning	1 pound pork shoulder, chopped
1½ teaspoons salt	1 pound veal shoulder, chopped
Dash pepper	5 to 6 strips bacon

Combine first 6 ingredients. Let stand 5 minutes. Add onion and meat and mix well. Line a loaf pan, 8 x 5 x 3 inches, with bacon strips, across the width of pan. Pack meat mixture into pan. Bake in moderate oven, 350°F., 1½ hours. Remove from oven. Invert meat loaf on baking sheet; raise oven temperature to very hot, 450°F. Return meat loaf to oven for about 10 minutes, to crisp bacon. Garnish with heated, canned broiled mushrooms, if desired. Makes 8 servings.

INDIVIDUAL MEAT LOAVES: Drain **1 No. 2 can tomatoes** (use liquid in another dish). Add pulp to 1½ **pounds chopped beef, salt and pepper** to taste, 1½ **cups soft bread crumbs, 1 egg,** beaten and **1 medium onion,** minced. Mix well. Pack in greased custard cups. Bake in moderately hot oven, 375°F., 50 minutes, or till brown. Serve with MUSHROOM SAUCE: blend and heat **1 can condensed mushroom soup** and **1/3 cup cream.** Makes 6 servings.

HAMBURGER GRILL

1 teaspoon salt	3/4 pound chopped beef
Dash pepper	2 large tomatoes,
2 tablespoons chopped onion	cut in halves, crosswise
1/4 cup evaporated milk	4 teaspoons mayonnaise
1/2 cup whole bran	Banana Scallops

Combine first 5 ingredients; let stand 5 minutes. Add beef; mix lightly. Form into 4 patties. Put in preheated broiler, 3 inches below heat, about 5 minutes. Turn. Top each tomato half with 1 teaspoon mayonnaise; broil with hamburgers 4 to 5 minutes. Serve with Banana Scallops. Makes 4 servings.

BANANA SCALLOPS

Heat **fat or salad oil**, 1 inch deep, in a skillet, to 375°F. Put **1/4 cup undiluted evaporated milk** in a bowl. Add **1½ teaspoons salt**; stir well. Peel **4 firm bananas**; cut crosswise in 3/4-inch pieces. Dip into milk. Drain. Roll in **1/2 cup fine corn flake crumbs**. Fry till brown, 1½ to 2 minutes. Drain well. Makes 4 servings.

SWEDISH MEAT BALLS

1 pound chopped beef	1/8 teaspoon pepper
1 cup soft bread crumbs	1/4 teaspoon nutmeg
1 cup milk	Fat
1 egg, well-beaten	1 cup hot water
2 medium onions, chopped	1 tablespoon flour
2 teaspoons salt	2 tablespoons cold water

Hot cooked rice

Put first 8 ingredients into a large bowl; mix thoroughly. Heat 2 tablespoons fat in a large skillet. Form meat mixture in 1-inch balls, using a teaspoon. Drop into skillet, a few at a time; brown on all sides. Remove and keep in a warm place. Continue till all meat balls are browned. Use more fat as needed.

Add hot water to drippings in skillet; bring to a boil. Blend flour with cold water. Stir into hot mixture; cook until thickened, stirring constantly. Return meat to skillet. Cover; simmer 30 minutes. Arrange rice around the edge of a flat serving dish. Pour meat balls and gravy in center. Makes 6 servings.

SPANISH STEAK: Pack **1½ pounds seasoned chopped beef** in greased 8 x 8 inch pan. Pour over **1 cup tomato sauce.** Top with **1/2 cup grated cheddar cheese, 12 stuffed olives,** sliced, **6 strips bacon.** Bake in hot oven, 400°F., 30 minutes. Makes 6 servings.

CHILI CON CARNE

3 tablespoons fat	1/2 teaspoon paprika
1 large onion, chopped	1/8 teaspoon cayenne
1 green pepper, chopped	1 bay leaf
1 pound chopped beef	1 tablespoon chili powder
1 No. 2 can (2½ cups) tomatoes	1 clove garlic, mashed
	1 teaspoon salt
1 10½- or 11-ounce can condensed tomato soup	1 No. 2 can (2½ cups) kidney beans

Heat fat in a large skillet. Add onion, green pepper, and meat. Cook until brown, stirring occasionally. Add next 6 ingredients. Cover. Simmer about 1 hour, stirring occasionally. Add additional water if mixture gets too thick. Combine garlic and salt. Add garlic mixture and beans to meat mixture. Stir well. Heat to boiling. Pour into a large serving bowl and garnish with **onion rings.** Serve with hot corn bread sticks. Makes 6 servings.

CORN STICKS: Generously grease 12 corn stick pans. Heat in oven while mixing batter. Beat **1 egg** in a bowl. Beat in **1½ cups butter-milk, 1/2 teaspoon baking soda, 1/2 cup sifted flour, 1½ cups corn meal, 1 teaspoon sugar, 1 tablespoon baking powder, 1 teaspoon salt, and 1/4 cup soft shortening.** Spoon into heated pans. Bake in hot oven, 450°F., 10 to 15 minutes. Makes 12 corn sticks.

POT ROAST WITH VEGETABLES

1 tablespoon fat
3- to 4-pound piece of beef,
   heel of round or rump
2 teaspoons salt
1/8 teaspoon pepper
1/3 cup cold water

1½ cups hot water
4 medium onions, peeled
8 small carrots, scraped
4 medium potatoes, pared
3 tablespoons flour

Heat fat in a large, heavy saucepot. Brown meat on all sides in fat. Sprinkle with salt and pepper; add hot water. Cover; simmer 2 hours, or till almost tender. Add onions; cook 10 minutes. Add carrots and potatoes; cook 30 to 35 minutes longer, or until tender. Remove meat and vegetables. Measure liquid in pan; add water, if necessary, to make 1½ cups. Bring to a boil. Blend flour and cold water; stir into liquid. Cook until thickened; stir constantly. Makes 4 servings with enough meat for a second meal.

POT ROAST—GINGERSNAP GRAVY: Combine **1/3 cup flour, 2 teaspoons salt, 1/4 teaspoon pepper,** and **1 teaspoon monosodium glutamate.** Dredge a **4- to 5-pound rump roast of beef** with this mixture. Heat **1/4 cup fat** in a large, heavy saucepot. Brown meat on all sides. Add **12 to 15 crushed gingersnaps** and **3 cups boiling water.** Cover; simmer 3 hours or until tender. Makes 8 to 10 servings.

BEEF STEW

2 pounds stewing beef—chuck, heel of round, or neck
Seasoned flour (salt and pepper added)
3 tablespoons fat
1 teaspoon salt
1/4 teaspoon pepper
1 teaspoon sugar
1 8-ounce can tomato sauce
5 cups boiling water
6 potatoes, pared
6 carrots, scraped
6 medium onions, peeled
1/4 teaspoon oregano or marjoram
2 cups cooked or canned peas

Cut beef in 1-inch cubes; dredge in flour. Heat fat in a large, heavy saucepot. Brown meat on all sides. Add salt, pepper, sugar, tomato sauce, and water. Simmer, covered 1½ hours, or until meat is almost tender.

Add potatoes, carrots, and onions; cover and cook another 30 minutes. Add oregano and peas. Cook an additional 15 minutes, or until meat and vegetables are done. If desired, thicken gravy before serving. To make gravy, blend **1/3 cup flour** and **1/3 cup water.** Stir into stew and cook until thickened. Makes 6 servings.

BURGUNDY BEEF STEW: For a de luxe stew, one you will be proud to serve to guests, try this. Reduce water to 4 cups. Add **1 cup Burgundy** with the tomato sauce and cook as directed above.

BREADED VEAL CUTLET

1 veal steak, 1 inch thick	1/2 cup fine dry bread crumbs
(about 2 pounds)	2 tablespoons fat or salad oil
1/2 cup buttermilk	1 cup tomato juice

Dip meat in buttermilk; coat with crumbs. Chill several hours. Heat fat in skillet. Brown meat on both sides. Add tomato juice. Cover; simmer 1 hour, or till tender. Add more tomato juice, if needed. Make pan gravy, if desired. Makes 6 servings.

SAVORY VEAL CUTLET

Cut **2 pounds veal cutlet** in serving-size pieces. Combine **1/4 cup salad oil, 1 tablespoon vinegar, 1 teaspoon salt, 1/2 teaspoon paprika, 1 bay leaf,** and **1 clove garlic,** mashed. Pour over meat; let stand about 4 hours; turn occasionally. Drain; save liquid. Heat **2 tablespoons fat** in a skillet; brown meat on both sides. Remove meat. Add **1/4 cup flour** to fat in skillet; stir till smooth. Add **1 cup water, 1 cup canned tomatoes, 1 teaspoon sugar,** and reserved oil mixture. Cook until thick; stir constantly. Add meat. Cover; simmer 1 hour, or till tender. Makes 6 servings.

ROAST PORK

Several cuts of pork are suitable for roasting—loin, fresh ham, shoulder, and pork butt. There are three kinds of loin roasts—blade loin, center loin, and the sirloin end. Shoulder, also called fresh picnic shoulder, can be purchased whole or in smaller roasts, boned and rolled.

Wipe meat with clean, damp cloth. Season with salt and pepper, if desired. Place, fat side up, on a rack in an open roaster or shallow baking pan. Roast in a moderate oven, 350°F., using the table below. Do not cover, add water, or baste. To insure best results, use a meat thermometer. Insert bulb so it rests in thickest part of meat without touching fat or bone. Thermometer should read 185°F., regardless of weight or type of roast.

Pork should always be well-done to develop the best flavor.

ROAST PORK TIMETABLE

Cut:	Weight:	Minutes per pound:
Loin	3 to 5 pounds	35 to 40
Fresh Ham	10 to 12 pounds	30 to 35
Shoulder		
Picnic (whole)	12 to 14 pounds	30 to 35
Boned and rolled	4 to 6 pounds	40 to 45
Pork Butt	4 to 6 pounds	45 to 50

STUFFED PORK CHOPS

6 thick pork chops
2 cups soft bread crumbs
1/4 cup melted butter
    or margarine
1/4 teaspoon salt

1/4 teaspoon poultry seasoning,
    sage, or thyme
2 tablespoons minced onion
Dash pepper
1/2 cup water

Make pockets in chops, by cutting a slit from fat side to bone. Combine next 6 ingredients. Fill pockets; fasten with toothpicks. Brown chops over low heat in a skillet. Season with additional salt and pepper. Add water. Cover and simmer 1 hour. Remove toothpicks. Arrange chops on a heated platter with **Bananas Sauté.** Make gravy, if desired, from pan drippings, a little **flour** and additional **water.** Makes 6 servings.

BANANAS SAUTÉ

Heat **1/3 cup butter or margarine** in a skillet. Peel **6 firm bananas.** Keep whole or cut in halves crosswise. Fry slowly until tender turning them to brown evenly. Sprinkle lightly with **salt.** Makes 6 servings.

BARBECUED SPARERIBS

2 pounds spareribs	1 tablespoon lemon juice
1 tablespoon butter or	1 tablespoon Worcestershire
margarine	1 tablespoon brown sugar
1/4 cup finely chopped onion	1/2 teaspoon dry mustard
1/2 cup water	1/2 teaspoon salt
1/2 cup ketchup	1/8 teaspoon pepper
1 tablespoon vinegar	1 No. 303 can sauerkraut

8 small potatoes, pared

Have spareribs cut in serving-size pieces; brown slowly in a large, heavy saucepot. Meanwhile, melt butter in skillet; add onion; cook until light brown. Add next 9 ingredients; simmer 20 minutes. Pour sauerkraut over spareribs; add sauce. Cover; simmer 1 hour. Add potatoes; cook 25 minutes or until tender. **Makes 4 servings.**

BAKED STUFFED SPARERIBS: Have **3 pounds spareribs** cut into 2 pieces of equal size. Prepare **1 package bread stuffing** according to directions; spread between the spareribs. Fasten together with string. Place in roasting pan; add **1/2 cup hot water;** cover. Roast in moderate oven, 350°F., 2½ hours, or till tender. Remove cover during last 1/2 hour. Makes 6 servings.

BAKED HAM

Place ham, fat side up, on rack in an open roaster or shallow baking pan. (Have ham at room temperature.) Bake in a moderately low oven, 325°F., using chart below. About 45 minutes before end of baking time, remove ham from oven. Slit rind with scissors, and peel off. If a glaze on the ham is desired, proceed as follows before returning it to the oven to finish baking.

TO GLAZE HAM: With a sharp knife make cuts 1/4-inch deep in fat in a diamond pattern. Stud with **whole cloves.** Make a paste of **1½ cups firmly packed brown sugar, 3 tablespoons prepared mustard,** and a **little water;** pat over surface. Bake 45 minutes longer, basting frequently with ham fat.

TIMETABLE FOR BAKING TENDER UNCOOKED HAM

Weight:	Minutes per pound (approximate):	Total Baking Time:
16 to 18 pounds	15	4 to 4½ hours
12 to 15 pounds	17	3½ to 4 hours
10 to 12 pounds	18	3 to 3½ hours
8 to 10 pounds	20	2¾ to 3 hours
5 to 8 pounds		
(half ham)	26	2¼ to 3 hours
(picnic ham)	35	3 to 4½ hours

ROAST LEG OF LAMB

Select a leg of lamb, 6 to 8 pounds. Allow 1/3 to 1/2 pound per serving. Wipe with a damp cloth. Do not remove the "fell" (thin, papery skin). Cut small gashes about 1 inch apart, lengthwise. Insert sliver of garlic in each gash. Place on a rack in an open roaster. Roast in low oven, 300°F., allowing 30 to 35 minutes per pound. Remove garlic after one hour. For unusual flavor, pour 1 cup unsweetened pineapple juice over the roast after garlic is removed. Baste 4 times. Serve with brown gravy.

BROWN GRAVY: Pour off all but **1/4 cup of fat** from pan drippings. Add **1/4 cup flour**; blend well. Cook over low heat till brown. Add **2 cups water** slowly; cook till thickened, stirring constantly. Add **salt and pepper** to taste. Makes about 2 cups.

ROAST STUFFED SHOULDER OF LAMB: Have a **4- to 5-pound shoulder lamb** boned to form a pocket. Combine **2/3 cup seedless raisins, 6 cups soft bread crumbs, 1 cup diced celery, 1/3 cup minced onion, 1/3 cup melted butter, 1/2 cup apricot nectar, 1 teaspoon salt, 2 teaspoons poultry seasoning, 2 beaten eggs**. Mix well. Fill pocket with half the mixture; sew. Roast on rack in open roaster in moderate oven, 350°F., 3 hours. Form remaining stuffing in patties; fry in **butter** till brown. Serve with roast. Makes 8 servings.

BROILED LAMB CHOPS

Lamb chops for broiling may be cut from 3/4 to 2 inches in thickness. Allow 1 to 2 loin or rib chops per person and 1 shoulder chop per person.

Preheat broiler. Put chops in broiler on a rack. Place thinner chops about 2 inches from the heat and thicker ones 3 inches from heat. Broil for half the time required. See timetable below. Season cooked side with salt and pepper. Turn and finish broiling. Lamb chops are always served well done.

BROILING TIMETABLE

Chops 3/4 inch thick	10 to 12 minutes
Chops 1 inch thick	14 to 16 minutes
Chops 1½ inches thick	16 to 18 minutes
Chops 2 inches thick	22 to 24 minutes

GRILLED TOMATOES (see picture above): Wash **6 firm medium tomatoes** and cut in halves, crosswise. Sprinkle with **salt and pepper.** Top each with **1 teaspoon mayonnaise.** Broil 2 to 3 inches from heat, 4 to 5 minutes. Sprinkle with **chopped parsley.** Makes 6 servings.
Note: These are excellent served with any chops or steaks and can be cooked with the meat during last few minutes of broiling.

LAMB STEW WITH DUMPLINGS

3 tablespoons fat
2½ pounds boned lamb, cut
    in 2-inch cubes
1 teaspoon salt
1/8 teaspoon pepper
Boiling water

8 small carrots, pared and cut in
    1-inch pieces
1 cup diced celery
1/2 cup diced onion
1½ teaspoons celery salt
1 recipe dumplings

Heat fat in a large, heavy saucepot. Add lamb. Brown on all sides. Add salt, pepper, and enough water to just cover meat. Bring to boil; lower heat; simmer 1 to 1½ hours, or until lamb is almost tender. Add vegetables and celery salt. Simmer 10 minutes longer. Add more salt and pepper if necessary.

Drop dumpling dough on stew by tablespoonfuls, being sure each spoonful rests on a piece of meat. Cook, uncovered, 10 minutes over low heat. Cover; cook 10 minutes longer. Serve in a heated bowl with dumplings on top. Makes 6 to 8 servings.

DUMPLINGS: Sift together into a bowl 1½ **cups sifted flour, 2 teaspoons baking powder** and **3/4 teaspoon salt**. Cut in **3 tablespoons shortening**. Stir in **3/4 cup milk**. Mix only until blended. Or, use **2 cups biscuit mix,** prepared according to package directions. Makes about 8 dumplings.

CURRIED LAMB

1½ tablespoons flour
1 teaspoon salt
1/2 teaspoon garlic salt
1½ pounds lamb shank, or
    shoulder, cut in 1-inch pieces
Butter or margarine
1 tablespoon curry powder

1 tablespoon sugar
2 medium onions, chopped
1 medium apple, pared,
    cored, and diced
3/4 cup hot water
Hot buttered rice
Paprika

Chutney, shredded coconut, peanuts, and raisins

Combine flour, salt, and garlic salt. Dredge lamb with flour mixture. Melt 2 tablespoons butter in a large skillet. Stir in curry powder and sugar; add onion and apple; cook over low heat 5 minutes or until onion is soft. Push to one side of skillet. Add more butter, if necessary, and brown lamb. Add water; cover. Simmer 1 hour or until tender. Add more water, if needed, during cooking, but sauce should be medium thick. Arrange rice in a border on a heated serving platter. Sprinkle with paprika. Pour meat mixture in center. Serve with chutney, shredded coconut, peanuts and raisins. Makes 4 to 6 servings.

SPANISH LAMB: Alternate layers of **Spanish Rice** and **sliced cooked lamb** in casserole. Top with **grated cheese.** Heat in moderate oven.

30

SHISH KEBAB

3/4 cup vinegar	1½ pounds lamb shoulder,
3/4 cup water	cut in 1-inch cubes
2 bay leaves	3 tomatoes, cut in sixths
1 teaspoon salt	18 small mushrooms
1 teaspoon sugar	6 slices bacon, cut in thirds

Combine vinegar, water, bay leaves, salt, and sugar in a small saucepan. Bring to a boil and simmer 5 minutes. Cool. Pour over lamb cubes in large bowl; marinate 24 hours. Drain; reserve marinade. Arrange meat, tomato wedges, mushrooms, and bacon slices alternately on 6 skewers. Broil 15 minutes, 3 to 4 inches from heat, in shallow pan. Turn frequently and baste with the reserved marinade. Makes 6 servings.

BEEF KEBAB

Beef may be substituted in place of lamb for this dish. Top round or sirloin are good cuts to use. Follow directions above.
Note: Other vegetables to use with the tomatoes and mushrooms are green peppers and onions.

SHEPHERD'S PIE

4 cups cubed left over roast beef, lamb, or veal
2 to 3 cups left over cooked vegetables*

2½ cups gravy
3 cups hot, mashed potatoes
1 egg, well-beaten

Heat meat, vegetables, and gravy to boiling. Pour into a 2-quart casserole. Combine potatoes and egg; mix thoroughly. Make a border around edge of casserole or cover top completely. Bake in hot oven, 425°F., 15 to 20 minutes or until brown. Makes 6 to 8 servings.

*You can use **1 No. 2 can or a 12-ounce package frozen mixed vegetables** and **1 cup canned onions.**

EMERGENCY GRAVY

When gravy from the roast runs short, try this. Use **condensed canned bouillon or bouillon cubes** (2 cubes to a cup of boiling water.) For each cup bouillon, use **2 tablespoons flour** mixed with **3 tablespoons cold water.** Stir into bouillon and cook until thickened. Season to taste.

Poultry Pointers

A plump bird on the table has a festive, prosperous air whether it be chicken or turkey. We think of it for Sunday dinner, for a company meal, as something sure to please.

HOW TO BUY CHICKEN

Now you can have "spring chicken" all the year 'round. If you prefer dark meat you can buy thighs and drumsticks only. Just know how to ask, and you'll get what you want.

Broilers-fryers are small, tender birds weighing 1½ to 3 pounds, whole, cut up, or in parts.

Roasters are tender, too, and weigh up to 5 pounds.

Stewing chickens are older, fatter, less tender birds weighing 2½ to 5 pounds. These are called fowls.

Capons are young, unsexed male birds, very tender, with a large proportion of white meat, weighing 5 pounds or more.

You can buy fresh **ready-to-cook** chickens of all types listed above. They have been cleaned, drawn, tagged with brand, and weighed. For **dressed** chicken, you pay for 25 to 30 percent waste because head, feet, and viscera have not been removed before pricing.

Quick-frozen chickens are ready to cook—cleaned and drawn. You can get roasters, broilers, fryers, and stewers, whole or cut-up. Or you can buy parts—breasts, drumsticks, wings, thighs, backs. Chicken livers, gizzards, and hearts are also packaged and quick-frozen. Defrost chicken, except stewers, completely before cooking.

Don't forget chicken in cans, ready-to-heat, packed whole, halved, or as boned meat, handy and delicious.

TURKEY

Not so long ago turkey was a holiday treat, served once or twice a year. Now the picture has changed, and turkey appears often on our tables. Half or quarter turkeys for small families and cut-up or by-the-piece turkey. Then there are small, young turkeys, weighing from 2 to 4 pounds for broiling or frying and the broad-breasted "apartment" size turkey.

Turkey is sold as "ready to cook", which means drawn and cleaned, either fresh or quick-frozen or "dressed", which means the turkey has not been drawn, and that head and feet are still on.

Quick-frozen turkeys must be completely defrosted before cooking. Leave it in the original mosture-vapor proof wrappng and defrost in the refrigerator. This takes 2 to 3 days depending on the size.

ROAST CHICKEN

PREPARATION FOR ROASTING: Remove pinfeathers with tweezers or catch between thumb and paring knife. Cut oil sack from top of tail. Singe, if necessary, to remove all hairs. Wash bird well, inside and out, under running cold water. Remove bits of lung and liver. Drain well and dry with paper towels. Wrap loosely in waxed paper and chill in the refrigerator until time for stuffing and roasting. Before stuffing, rub inside lightly with salt.

STUFFING AND TRUSSING: Fill the neck cavity lightly with stuffing and fasten neck skin to the back of the bird with skewers or wooden picks. Fold wings akimbo with wing tips under the bird. Pack the body cavity loosely with stuffing. Lace opening wth skewers or wooden picks and string. Tie the legs together and fasten to the tail. Stuff bird just before roasting.

ROASTING: Rub skin generously with softened or melted unsalted shortening. Place bird, breast side up,* on a rack in a shallow baking pan or open roaster. Cover with a double thickness of cheese-cloth dipped in melted shortening. Roast according to ROAST CHICKEN TIMETABLE (see p. 35). Baste frequently with pan drippings or additional shortening. Bird is done when the meat on the leg can be easily pierced with a fork.

*OR, roast, breast side down, in a V-shaped rack. Cover with

cheesecloth as above. When the bird is about half done turn right side up to brown breast. Continue as above, basting frequently.

Plan to have the bird done about 20 minutes before serving. This allows time for making gravy and removing the skewers.

ROAST CHICKEN TIMETABLE
(For chilled stuffed chicken)

Weight stuffed:*	Total hours (approximate):	Oven Temperature:
3½ to 4 pounds	2 to 2¾	350°F.
4 to 5 pounds	2½ to 3	325°F.
5 to 6 pounds	3 to 3½	325°F.

*Approximately equal to purchase weight of a New York or market dressed chicken—plucked but not drawn, head and feet on.

CREAM GRAVY

Pour drippings (fat and meat juices) from the pan. Skim off the fat. For each cup of gravy desired, use **1½ tablespoons fat, 1½ tablespoons flour,** and **1 cup meat juices and thin cream.**

Measure fat back into the roasting pan; add the flour. Cook over low heat until frothy, stirring constantly. Scrape down browned particles left in pan after roasting. For a darker gravy, let fat mixture brown slightly. Add liquid all at once. Cook, stirring constantly, until thickened. Simmer about 5 minutes.

MILK GRAVY: Use **milk** in place of cream in the above recipe.

TIPS FOR STUFFING

Bread for stuffing should be at least 1 day old. Remove crusts and cut into 1/4-inch or 1/2-inch cubes, or tear into crumbs with a fork. A pound loaf makes about 8 cups of cubes or crumbs.

Plan about 3/4 cup of cubes for each pound of bird. Pack stuffing loosely. If packed tightly, it becomes heavy and soggy.

Ingredients may be prepared and measured in advance. However, combine them just before stuffing. Roast bird at once.

Stuffing left over after filling the bird can be baked in a covered casserole during the last half hour of roasting.

When you use the giblets in stuffing, cook immediately after cleaning. Cover gizzard and heart with water; add 1/4 teaspoon salt, and a bay leaf. Simmer, covered, 2 to 2½ hours or until tender. Add liver last 15 minutes of cooking. Cool and cut very fine. Save broth to use in stuffing or gravy.

BREAD STUFFING

1/3 cup butter or margarine
1/4 cup chopped onion
1/3 cup chopped celery
1/2 teaspoon salt
Dash pepper

1/4 teaspoon poultry seasoning
Giblets, cooked and chopped
3 to 4 cups soft bread crumbs
   or cubes
Stock from giblets or milk

Melt butter in a skillet. Add onion and celery and cook over low heat until tender but not brown. Add seasoning and giblets. Pour over bread crumbs and toss lightly. If a moist stuffing is desired, add stock from giblets or milk. Makes enough stuffing for a 4- to 5-pound chicken. Double the recipe for an 8- to 10-pound turkey; triple it for a turkey 12 to 16 pounds.

Note: Packaged, prepared bread crumbs may be used in place of soft. It will be necessary to increase the quantity of liquid.

CHESTNUT RICE STUFFING

1 4-ounce can mushroom pieces
1/2 cup butter or margarine
1/4 cup chopped ripe olives
2 tablespoons chopped parsley
1/4 cup chopped celery

1½ cups boiled chestnuts,
   mashed
1½ cups cooked rice
1/4 cup milk
Salt and pepper to taste

Drain mushrooms; reserve liquid. Heat butter in a skillet. Sauté mushrooms, olives, parsley, and celery. Combine mushroom mixture with reserved liquid and remaining ingredients. Mix well. Makes enough stuffing for a 5- to 6-pound chicken or half a turkey.

MUSHROOM STUFFING

2 4-ounce cans mushrooms
   (sliced or pieces)
1 cup butter or margarine
1/2 cup finely chopped onion
3 quarts soft bread crumbs

1 cup finely diced celery
1/4 cup chopped parsley
1½ teaspoons salt
1/4 teaspoon pepper
1 tablespoon poultry seasoning

Drain mushrooms; save liquid. Melt butter in a deep kettle. Add mushrooms and onion; cook until onion is tender but not brown. Add remaining ingredients plus mushroom liquid. Mix lightly. Makes enough stuffing for a 15-pound turkey.

FRIED CHICKEN

2½- to 3-pound chicken, cut up
1/2 cup fat
2 tablespoons butter or margarine

1/2 cup flour
1½ teaspoons salt
1/4 cup water

Wash chicken and dry with paper towels. Melt fat and butter over low heat in chicken fryer or large skillet. Combine flour and salt in a sturdy paper bag. Place 3 or 4 pieces of chicken in the bag. Shake to coat the chicken. Put chicken into hot fat. Repeat until all chicken is floured. Fry over low heat until browned on one side; turn to brown on all sides evenly. Add water. Cover, simmer 30 minutes, adding a little more water, if necessary. Uncover; cook 15 minutes longer. Makes 4 servings.

MARYLAND FRIED CHICKEN

Have **2 fryers** cut up at market; dredge with **seasoned flour** (see **Fried Chicken**, above). Fry slowly in **fat,** 1 inch deep, in 2 covered skillets until brown and tender, about 30 minutes; turn occasionally. Remove to platter; keep warm. Make cream gravy with fat left in skillets; add chopped cooked giblets if desired. Pour over chicken.

PIQUANT BROILED CHICKEN

1 2- to 2½-pound broiling
    chicken, cut in quarters
1/2 cup salad oil
3 tablespoons vinegar

1/4 teaspoon dry mustard
1/2 teaspoon salt
1/4 teaspoon paprika
1/2 clove garlic, peeled and minced

Wash chicken; dry with paper towels. Place in a shallow pan. Combine remaining ingredients. Pour over chicken. Let stand in refrigerator at least 1 hour; turn chicken once. Remove chicken from marinade. Place, skin side down, on broiler rack. Put in preheated broiler 5 to 8 inches from heat. Broil 12 minutes, basting often with marinade. Turn; broil 15 minutes longer, or till chicken is tender, continuing to baste. Makes 4 servings.

LEMON-BROILED CHICKEN: Wash a 1½- to 2-pound broiling chicken, cut in half. Dry with paper towels. Put in a shallow pan. Combine 1/4 cup salad oil, 1/4 cup lemon juice, 2 tablespoons grated onion, 1/2 teaspoon salt, and 1/4 teaspoon pepper. Pour over chicken. Let stand in refrigerator at least 4 hours; turn once. Remove chicken from marinade. Place, skin side down, on broiler rack. Put in preheated broiler, about 5 inches from heat. Broil 12 minutes; baste 2 or 3 times with marinade. Turn; broil 12 minutes longer or until tender. Makes 2 servings.

OLD-FASHIONED CHICKEN PIE

1 fowl, cut up (about 5 pounds)
3 cups water
1 medium onion, peeled and sliced
Handful of celery tops
1 tablespoon salt
1/4 teaspoon pepper
1 bay leaf

1/2 cup flour
1⅔ cups undiluted,
    evaporated milk
2 cups cooked, sliced carrots
1 pound cooked small
    white onions
Recipe Baking Powder biscuits

Place chicken in large kettle with next 6 ingredients. Cover; bring to boiling. Simmer 1½ to 2 hours, or until tender. Remove chicken from broth; cool. Strain broth; cool. Remove chicken from bones; cut into bite-size pieces.

Skim fat from broth; measure 1/2 cup fat and 2⅓ cups broth. (Use any remaining broth in soup.) Heat the 1/2 cup fat in large saucepan; blend in flour; stir in the 2⅓ cups broth and milk. Cook, stirring constantly, until sauce thickens; boil 1 minute. Add chicken, carrots, and onions, and salt and pepper, if needed. Reheat. Pour into a 3-quart baking dish. Arrange uncooked baking powder biscuits over top. Bake in very hot oven, 450°F., 20 to 25 minutes, or until biscuits brown. Makes 6 to 8 servings.

Note: See p. 79 for recipe for Baking Powder Biscuits or use packaged biscuit mix. Just for fun, use chicken-shaped cutter.

CHICKEN FRICASSEE

1 4- to 5-pound fowl, cut up	1 tablespoon salt
3 cups hot water	1 bay leaf
1 onion, studded with a few	1 carrot, cut in chunks
whole cloves	6 tablespoons flour
3 stalks celery, with leaves	1/2 cup milk or cream

Simmer chicken with water, onion, celery, salt, bay leaf and carrot until tender, 3 to 4 hours (or use pressure cooker according to directions). Remove chicken to a heated serving dish; keep warm. Strain broth; skim off excess fat. Measure 3 cups broth, adding water if necessary. Mix flour and milk to smooth paste; add slowly to broth; cook over low heat, stirring, until thickened. Season to taste with additional salt and pepper; pour over chicken. Serve with hot baking powder biscuits, if desired. (See p. 79.) Makes 5 to 6 servings.

BROWN FRICASSEE OF CHICKEN: Wash and dry a **4- to 5-pound fowl**, cut up. Combine **1/2 cup flour, 1 teaspoon salt,** and **dash pepper** in paper bag. Place 2 or 3 chicken pieces in the bag; shake until well-coated. Continue until all pieces are coated. Fry in deep kettle over low heat in **1/4 cup fat or salad oil** until brown on all sides. Continue as above, adding water, onion, etc. to kettle in which chicken was browned.

CHICKEN TETRAZZINI

1 3- to 4-pound chicken, cut-up	2 tablespoons flour
2 stalks celery, with leaves	1/2 pound mushrooms, sliced
1 medium onion, sliced	1 egg yolk, slightly beaten
1½ teaspoons salt	3 tablespoons cream
Boiling water	1 8-ounce package green noodles
1/4 cup chicken fat, butter,	2 to 3 tablespoons grated
or margarine	Parmesan cheese

1 teaspoon butter or margarine

Put chicken, celery, onion, and 1 teaspoon of the salt in a kettle. Add water to cover. Simmer till tender (about 1½ hours). Remove chicken; strain broth. Chill chicken and broth. Remove skin and bones from chicken; leave meat in fairly large pieces. Skim fat from broth. Measure 2 tablespoons of the fat or butter into saucepan; blend in flour and remaining salt. Add 1 cup of the broth. Cook over low heat, stirring, until thickened. Cook mushrooms in remaining 2 tablespoons fat till brown. Combine egg yolk and cream. Stir slowly into sauce. Add chicken and mushrooms; heat to serving temperature. Meanwhile cook noodles in remaining broth, adding water if necessary; drain. Arrange in shallow baking dish; pour chicken mixture over noodles. Sprinkle with cheese; dot with butter. Brown under broiler. Makes 4 to 5 servings.

MEXICAN CHICKEN WITH FRUITS

1 4-pound chicken, cut up
2 cups boiling water
2 tablespoons chili powder
1/4 teaspoon pepper
1/4 teaspoon cinnamon
2 tablespoons grated onion
1 teaspoon monosodium glutamate
1 teaspoon salt

1/4 cup fat or drippings
2 cups unsweetened pineapple
    juice, canned or frozen
2 cups pineapple chunks,
    canned or frozen
2 fully ripe bananas, sliced
    lengthwise
1 ripe avocado, sliced

1/2 pound white grapes

Put chicken in a deep kettle; add next 7 ingredients. Cover; simmer 1 hour. Remove chicken from broth. Reserve broth. Heat fat in a skillet. Brown chicken on all sides; arrange in baking pan. Add pineapple juice to broth; heat and pour over chicken. Arrange pineapple chunks over chicken. Bake in moderately hot oven, 375°F., 30 minutes. Lift chicken and fruit into a serving dish; garnish with the fruit. Serve gravy separately. Makes 6 servings.

CHICKEN ESPAGNOLE: Put a **cut-up fowl** in kettle. Heat **1/4 cup fat;** blend in **1/2 cup flour.** Add **3/4 cup ketchup, 3 cups water, 1 teaspoon salt, dash Tabasco, juice of 1 lemon.** Bring to a boil; pour over fowl. Cover; simmer 3 hours. Makes 6 servings.

ROAST TURKEY

WHOLE TURKEY: Prepare for stuffing and roasting in the same way as chicken. See pp. 34-36. Use the table below for roasting.

HALF TURKEY: Wash, clean, and dry the turkey. Rub cut side with salt. Skewer skin to breast meat. Tie the leg to the tail.

Place, cut side down, on a rack in a shallow baking pan. Brush with melted shortening and cover with cheesecloth dipped in melted shortening. Roast in a moderately low oven, 325°F., allowing 25 to 30 minutes per pound. Baste frequently.

Make a mound of stuffing, the approximate shape of the cavity, on heavy waxed paper. When bird is half done, remove from oven. Place paper with dressing on the rack. Place turkey over dressing and roast till done.

ROAST TURKEY TIMETABLE
(For chilled stuffed turkey)

Weight stuffed:	Total hours (approximate):	Oven Temperature:
4 to 6 pounds	2¾ to 3½	325°F.
6 to 8 pounds	3½ to 4	325°F.
8 to 12 pounds	4 to 4½	325°F.
12 to 16 pounds	4½ to 5	325°F.
16 to 20 pounds	5½ to 7	325°F.
20 to 24 pounds	7 to 8½	325°F.

HAWAIIAN TURKEY CURRY

2 cups coconut milk
1/2 cup minced onion
1/3 cup butter or margarine
1/3 cup flour
4 teaspoons curry powder
1 teaspoon salt
1/2 teaspoon monosodium
    glutamate

1/4 teaspoon ginger
2 cups turkey broth
3 cups diced cooked turkey
1 cup cubed pineapple,
    fresh or canned
Hot cooked rice
Chutney, raisins, shredded
    coconut, and peanuts

Prepare coconut milk as directed below, if fresh is not obtainable. Cook onion in butter until soft but not brown. Blend in flour, curry powder, salt, monosodium glutamate, and ginger. Add coconut milk and broth all at once. Cook over low heat, stirring constantly, until thickened. Add turkey and pineapple. Heat thoroughly. Serve with the hot rice, chutney, raisins, shredded coconut, and peanuts. Makes 6 to 8 servings.

COCONUT MILK: Pour **2 cups hot milk** over **4 cups grated fresh coconut or contents of 2 packages or cans of shredded coconut.** Let stand 30 minutes. Strain through double cheesecloth, pressing to remove all liquid. Discard coconut. Chill coconut milk until ready to use. Makes 2 cups.

Fish is Fine Fare

—for Friday or any other day, if it is perfectly cooked. Over-cooking is the great fault, and many people don't like fish and seafood because they've never had it any other way. A pity!

With modern refrigerated transportation, air freight and quick-freezing, there is little or no danger of spoilage between the time a fish is drawn from the water and the time it is sold to you. Once you get it home, pop it into the refrigerator and cook it the same day, if possible, for finest flavor. If the fish is frozen, de-frost it just before cooking.

HOW TO BUY FISH

If you are buying fresh fish, look at its eyes. If they are sunken you can be sure that fish is not strictly fresh—buy one with bright, bulging eyes instead. Then sniff. Any fisherman will tell you that a truly fresh fish has no odor. And who is a better authority?

Buy fish that makes the least work for you—filleted, cut into steaks, or whole fish dressed at the market. Ask the dealer to remove the blood line under the backbone, so that the fish will stay fresh and sweet.

Fillets are boneless, solid slices cut away from the sides of the fish. If the skin is left on, the cooked fish will be juicier and have more flavor.

Steaks are cross section cuts of large fish like cod, swordfish or salmon, and have few or no bones.

Dressed fish has had fins, entrails, tail and scales removed; the head, too, if you prefer, except for small fish like brook trout.

Quick-frozen fish and seafoods need no preparation other than cooking, and there is no waste involved. For best results, follow de-frosting and cooking instructions on the package.

HOW TO CLEAN A FISH

If the man of the house is a fisherman, and he brings his catch home for you to clean, here's how to do it:

Lay the fish on a large sheet of paper. Working from the tail toward the head, scrape off the scales with a fish scaler or sharp knife. Cut around the back fins and pull them out. Or cut off the fins with scissors. Leave a small part visible so the bones can be easily located after the fish is cooked.

Cut a gash in the abdomen with scissors or a sharp knife and remove the entrails. Remove the blood line in the abdominal cavity under the backbone with the tip of a knife. Wash and dry the fish and store in the refrigerator until cooking time.

Try the very special fish recipes that follow—and don't wait for Friday!

FRIED FISH FILLETS

2 pounds fish fillets—cod, flounder,
    sole or haddock
1 teaspoon salt
1 egg, slightly beaten

1 tablespoon milk or water
1 cup fine dry bread
    crumbs or cornmeal
Fat or salad oil

Wash fish and dry with paper towels. Cut into serving-size pieces. Sprinkle with salt. Combine egg and milk in a flat dish. Dip fish in egg mixture, then in crumbs.

Heat fat in skillet. The fat should be about 1/8 inch deep. Fry fish over medium heat. When brown on one side, turn carefully; brown other side. Cook about 5 minutes on each side. Drain on absorbent paper or paper towels. Serve with Tartar Sauce, if desired, or lemon slices. Makes 6 servings.

TARTAR SAUCE

Combine 1 cup mayonnaise, 1 teaspoon Worcestershire, 2 teaspoons finely chopped onion, 2 tablespoons chopped dill pickle, 2 tablespoons chopped stuffed olives, 2 teaspoons chopped parsley and blend well. Makes about 1¼ cups.

BAKED STUFFED SEA BASS

1 4- to 5-pound sea bass, dressed	1 small onion, grated
3/4 cup melted butter or margarine	1/2 teaspoon rosemary
1/2 package prepared bread stuffing	1/4 teaspoon oregano

Wash fish and dry with paper towels. Combine 1/2 cup of the butter with remaining ingredients. Mix well. Fill fish cavity 2/3 full. Close opening with wooden picks laced together with string. Cut 3 or 4 gashes through skin, on each side and brush with butter.

Line a shallow baking pan with aluminum foil. Put fish in pan. Bake in hot oven, 400°F., 30 to 45 minutes or till tender. Baste occasionally with butter. Put on a heated platter. Serve with Lobster Sauce. Makes 6 servings.

LOBSTER SAUCE: Melt **2 tablespoons butter or margarine**. Blend in **1 tablespoon flour, 1 teaspoon salt, dash pepper**, and **few drops Tabasco**. Combine **1 cup light cream** and **1/2 cup milk**; add to flour mixture. Stir over low heat until slightly thickened. Pour some of the hot sauce into **1 slightly beaten egg**; blend; return to hot sauce. Add **1½ cups lobster meat**, cooked or canned, **2 tablespoons minced parsley**, and **2 tablespoons dry sherry**. Heat but do not allow to boil. Makes 6 servings.

BROILED SWORDFISH

2 pounds swordfish steaks, cut   **1 teaspoon monosodium glutamate**
1 inch thick   **Salt and pepper**
Melted butter or margarine

Sprinkle fish with monosodium glutamate. Let stand 5 minutes. Sprinkle with salt and pepper. Brush with melted butter. Place on greased broiler rack in broiler, about 3 inches from heat. Broil about 8 minutes on each side, brushing frequently with melted butter. Arrange on a heated platter; garnish with lemon slices, if desired. Makes 6 servings.

FISH FILLETS LOUISIANA

Beat **1 egg;** add **1/4 teaspoon salt, 1 teaspoon curry powder, 1 tablespoon chopped parsley, 1 cup flaked salmon (a 7¾-ounce can),** and **1½ cups cooked rice.** Mix lightly. Spread on **3 fish fillets.** Top with **3 more fish fillets.** Tie securely with string. Place in a greased shallow baking dish; dot with **3 tablespoons butter or margarine.** Pour **1 cup milk** into baking dish. Bake in moderate oven, 350°F., 30 minutes. Makes 6 servings.

BROILED SALMON STEAKS

Grease broiler pan or line with aluminum foil and grease it. Heat pan in broiler. Wipe **4 salmon steaks,** 1 inch thick, with damp clean cloth; sprinkle lightly with **salt, pepper,** and **paprika;** place on broiler pan. Broil with fish 3 inches from heat, turning once, 8 to 10 minutes, or until fish flakes easily. Place on heated platter; serve with Cucumber Sauce. Makes 4 servings.

CUCUMBER SAUCE

1 cup diced cucumber	**1 teaspoon grated lemon rind**
Water	**1 teaspoon grated onion**
2 tablespoons butter	**1/2 teaspoon salt**
or margarine	**1/2 teaspoon monosodium**
2 tablespoons flour	**glutamate**
2 teaspoons lemon juice	**Dash pepper**

Cook cucumber in 1/2 cup water until tender; drain, saving cooking water. Melt butter; blend in flour. Measure cooking water; add enough more water to make 1 cup; add to flour mixture. Cook until thickened, stirring constantly. Add remaining ingredients; blend well. Add cooked cucumber. Makes about 2 cups.

BROILED BROOK TROUT

Wash **drawn brook trout** in cold water. Dry with paper towels. Brush inside and out with **melted butter or margarine.** Sprinkle with **salt and pepper.**

Grease a shallow baking pan well, or line with aluminum foil and grease the foil. Put fish in pan. Broil 3 inches from heat for 5 minutes. Turn and broil 4 to 5 minutes longer. Brush with **melted butter or margarine** several times during cooking. Serve with Tartar Sauce, if desired. (see p. 46.)

BAKED FISH FILLETS ESPAGNOLE

6 individual fish fillets
4 tablespoons fat or salad oil
4 tablespoons flour
1 onion, minced

2 cups canned tomato sauce
1/2 cup chopped green olives
1 teaspoon salt
1/8 teaspoon pepper

Brown fish fillets in 2 tablespoons of the fat. Place in a shallow baking dish. Heat remaining fat in saucepan. Add flour, blend. Add onion, tomato sauce, olives, salt, and pepper. Pour over fish. Bake in hot oven, 400°F., 30 minutes, or until fish flakes easily with a fork. Makes 6 servings.

FRENCH FRIED SHRIMP

2 pounds raw large shrimp   **1 teaspoon salt**
2 eggs, beaten   **Dash pepper**
1/4 cup flour   **Fat or salad oil**

Remove shells from shrimp, using a sharp paring knife. Lift out the vein which runs along the back. Wash in cold water. Dry on paper towels. In bowl, combine egg with next 3 ingredients; beat until smooth. Add shrimp.

Heat fat in a deep fryer or kettle. Have fat 2 to 3 inches deep. Heat to 375°F. on a fat thermometer or until a 1-inch cube of bread browns in about 40 seconds. Using fork, place shrimp into fat, one at a time; fry until golden brown, 3 to 5 minutes. Drain on paper towels. Serve with Tartar Sauce, if desired (see p. 46). Makes 8 servings.

BUTTERFLY SHRIMP

Shell and clean shrimp, leaving tails on. Split shrimp, cutting deeply, almost to inner edge. Open, then press flat with bottom of measuring cup. Prepare batter as above; add shrimp. Fry, until brown. Serve with soy sauce or chutney.

BROILED LOBSTER

Order **lobster** split lengthwise and cleaned, with large claws cracked. Allow 3/4 to 1 pound lobster in shell per serving.

Brush with **melted butter or margarine**. Sprinkle with **salt, pepper,** and **minced parsley**. Place, meat side up, on broiler rack, 3 to 4 inches from heat. Broil 12 to 14 minutes for small lobsters; 16 to 18 minutes for larger ones. If you broil several at a time, cut off large claws; arrange around the sides of the broiler pan, with body sections in center. Serve with **melted butter or margarine** and **lemon wedges**.

LOBSTER SHORTCAKE

2 cups cooked or canned   2 cups hot medium white sauce
lobster meat   6 hot baking powder biscuits
6 slices American cheese

Add lobster to white sauce; stir lightly. Arrange 6 biscuit halves on heat-proof platter. Pour creamed lobster over biscuits. Top with remaining biscuit halves. Top each with slice of cheese; broil slowly until cheese melts. Makes 6 servings.

DEVILED CRABMEAT

2 6½-ounce cans crabmeat,
 drained and boned
1 small onion, minced
5 tablespoons butter or margarine
2 tablespoons flour
1 teaspoon dry mustard
1 cup milk

1/2 teaspoon salt
1/4 teaspoon pepper
2 sprigs parsley, chopped
1/2 teaspoon nutmeg
1 egg, beaten
1 cup grated sharp cheddar
 cheese

1/2 cup dry bread crumbs

Flake crabmeat; set aside. Cook onion in 3 tablespoons of the butter until tender but not brown. Remove from heat; stir in flour and mustard until well blended. Add milk; stir until smooth. Return to heat; cook, stirring constantly until thick, about 2 minutes. Add salt, pepper, parsley, and nutmeg. Stir a little of the sauce into the egg; add egg mixture to remaining hot sauce. Stir constantly until boiling starts. Remove from heat before sauce boils; stir in cheese and crabmeat. Turn into individual ramekins or shells.

Melt remaining 2 tablespoons butter. Stir in the dry bread crumbs. Sprinkle over crabmeat. Bake in a hot oven, 400°F., about 10 minutes or until brown. Makes 4 to 6 servings.

Note: You can use 2 cups fresh crabmeat, in place of the canned.

SHRIMP JAMBALAYA

1 to 1½ **pounds cleaned cooked shrimp,**
    fresh or frozen
4 **tablespoons butter or**
    margarine

3 **firm bananas**
Salt
3 **cups hot cooked rice**
2 **cups Creole Sauce**

Heat shrimp in the top of a double boiler over hot water. Melt butter or margarine in large frying pan. Peel bananas, and cut crosswise into halves. Fry bananas slowly in butter until tender, and are easily pierced with a fork, turning to brown evenly. Sprinkle lightly with salt.

Make a bed of the rice on a large heated platter. Arrange bananas around edge and shrimp on top. Pour over part of the sauce. Serve remainder on the side. Makes 6 servings.

CREOLE SAUCE: Heat **1/3 cup fat or salad oil;** add **1 green pepper,** thinly sliced, **1 onion,** thinly sliced, and **1 clove garlic.** Cover; cook until tender but not brown. Add **1/4 teaspoon chili powder, 1 teaspoon sugar, 1 teaspoon salt, 1/4 teaspoon pepper,** and **2 cups canned tomatoes.** Cook over low heat for 30 minutes, stirring occasionally. Mix **2 tablespoons cornstarch** with **2 tablespoons water;** stir into sauce. Cook about 5 minutes, stirring constantly until thick. Remove garlic before serving. Makes about 2 cups.

The Macaroni Family

"Stuck a feather in his cap
And called it—Macaroni"
YANKEE DOODLE

This two-century-old song was by way of being prophetic, for today macaroni is as American as Yankee Doodle for all its ancient origin.

Do you think of macaroni as Italian? Actually the Chinese were eating—and writing about macaroni products as early as 5000 B.C.! And to a thirteenth century king goes the honor of naming this food. When he tasted it he exclaimed, "Ma Caroni!" which meant, "How very dear."

Italians call it "pasta"—we group all members of this big family under the name macaroni, whatever the size or shape. Spaghetti, egg noodles, shells, alphabets, bowknots, stars, lasagne, noodles—the complete list is too long to include here—provide wonderful bases for a bewildering variety of delicious dishes. In this selection you will find a group of our favorites. Others are included elsewhere in the book.

HOW TO COOK MACARONI

Some like macaroni quite tender, others prefer it firm or "al dente" as the Italians say. As a general rule, cooking directions on the package should be followed, but do avoid overcooking.

To cook 8 ounces of macaroni, add 1 tablespoon of salt to 3 quarts of boiling water. Add the macaroni slowly, so that the water does not stop boiling. Cook uncovered, stirring occasionally with a long-handled fork to prevent sticking, until macaroni is tender. (One Italian chef we know always adds about a tablespoon of cooking oil to the water to keep strands separate.)

When the macaroni is done, drain it **at once** in a colander or large sieve. Modern macaroni products do not need rinsing. (Our same chef always dashes a cup of cold water into the pot as he turns off the heat, to stop cooking immediately.)

HOW MUCH TO COOK

Macaroni and spaghetti double in volume when cooked. Egg noodles do not increase in bulk. Eight ounces of macaroni and spaghetti will make six servings after cooking. The same weight of egg noodles will make four servings.

MACARONI WITH MEAT SAUCE

2 tablespoons fat or
  salad oil
1/2 cup chopped onion
1 garlic clove, minced
1 pound chopped beef
1 No. 2 can (2½ cups) tomatoes
1 cup diced celery
1/2 cup diced green pepper

1½ teaspoons salt
1/4 teaspoon celery salt
Few drops Tabasco
1 teaspoon Worcestershire
1 4-ounce can mushrooms
1 8-ounce package elbow macaroni,
  cooked
1 tablespoon chopped parsley

Grated Parmesan cheese

Heat fat or salad oil; add onion and garlic; cook until onion is soft but not brown. Add beef; cook and stir until lightly browned. Add next 7 ingredients. Bring to boil. Cover; simmer 45 minutes. Add mushrooms; heat to boiling. Arrange macaroni on a large, heated serving platter. Pour meat mixture over macaroni. Sprinkle with parsley and cheese. Makes 6 servings.

MACARONI CUES: When cooking any macaroni product, add 2 tablespoons cooking oil to the water to keep pieces from sticking together. A little shortening rubbed around the inside rim of the kettle keeps macaroni from boiling over during cooking.

BAKED MACARONI AND CHEESE

1 8-ounce package elbow macaroni	Dash pepper
Boiling water	2 cups milk
Salt	2 cups grated sharp cheddar cheese
3 tablespoons butter or margarine	1 tablespoon grated onion
2 tablespoons flour	1/2 tablespoon dry mustard
	1 teaspoon Worcestershire
	1/2 cup buttered crumbs
Crisp bacon strips	

Cook macaroni in boiling, salted water according to package directions. Drain. Melt butter; blend in flour, 1 teaspoon salt, and pepper. Add milk; cook over low heat until smooth and thickened, stirring constantly. Add cheese, onion, mustard, and Worcestershire; continue to cook until cheese melts. Add macaroni. Pour into a greased 2-quart casserole. Top with crumbs. Bake in moderate oven, 375°F., about 25 minutes or until browned. Garnish with bacon. Makes 6 to 8 servings.

CURRIED MACARONI: Cook an **8-ounce package elbow macaroni or macaroni shells.** Prepare **2 cups medium white sauce.** Add **1 tablespoon each minced onion and curry powder.** Add cooked macaroni; heat thoroughly. Makes 6 servings.

ITALIAN SPAGHETTI

2 tablespoons fat	1 bay leaf
1 pound chopped beef	2 teaspoons sugar
1 large onion, chopped	1 clove garlic, mashed
1 small green pepper, chopped	2 teaspoons salt
1 6-ounce can tomato paste	Boiling water
1 No. 2 can (2½ cups) tomatoes	1 8-ounce package spaghetti
1/2 cup water	Grated Parmesan cheese

Heat fat in a large skillet. Brown meat. Break into small pieces with the side of a spoon as it browns. Add onion and green pepper; cook about 10 minutes, or until tender. Stir in next 5 ingredients. Cover; simmer about 1 hour, stirring occasionally.

Mix garlic and 1 teaspoon of the salt. Stir into sauce. If a more highly seasoned sauce is desired, add a few drops **Tabasco**. Add remaining salt to water. Cook spaghetti according to package directions. To serve, arrange spaghetti on a heated platter, pour sauce over it and sprinkle with cheese. Makes 4 to 6 servings.

VIENNESE SPAGHETTI: Cut **Vienna sausages from two 4-ounce cans** in 1/2 inch slices; combine with contents of **two 1-pound cans of spaghetti;** pour into casserole. Top with **1/2 cup buttered crumbs.** Bake in moderate oven, 350°F., 20 minutes. Makes 6 servings.

SPAGHETTI WITH MEAT BALLS

1½ pounds chopped beef
1 medium onion, grated
1/3 cup finely chopped parsley
1 egg
1 slice of bread, coarsely crumbled
3/4 teaspoon salt
Dash pepper

1/4 teaspoon marjoram
2 8-ounce cans
   tomato sauce
1 small onion, grated
Dash curry powder
Dash ground cloves
1/4 teaspoon salt

Hot cooked spaghetti

Combine first 8 ingredients in medium bowl; toss together lightly with a fork. Set aside. Mix next 5 ingredients in a large skillet; heat to boiling, stirring often. Turn heat low. Form seasoned meat mixture into bite-size balls; drop each into sauce when shaped. Heat sauce to boiling; simmer over low heat 10 minutes, or just until cooked to desired doneness. Stir occasionally. Serve piping hot, with spaghetti. Makes 8 servings.

HALF-HOUR SPAGHETTI SAUCE: Mince **1 garlic clove**; chop **1 medium onion**; brown in **2 tablespoons salad oil**. Add **1 pound chopped beef**; cook till brown. Add **1 can tomato soup**, a **6-ounce can tomato paste**, **1/2 cup water**, **1/4 teaspoon oregano**. Simmer 1/2 hour. Serve on cooked spaghetti. Makes 6 servings.

TUNA FILLED CHEESE-NOODLE RING

1 8-ounce package wide noodles	1 cup milk
Boiling water	3 eggs, well-beaten
Salt	2 cups grated sharp Cheddar cheese
	Dash pepper

Break noodles in 1-inch pieces; cook in boiling, salted water according to package directions. Drain. Scald milk; pour into eggs gradually; stir constantly. Add to noodles with 1½ cups of the cheese, 1 teaspoon salt, and pepper. Mix well. Spoon into well-greased 10-inch ring mold. Set mold in pan of hot water. Bake in a moderately low oven, 325°F., 45 minutes. Unmold on baking sheet. Sprinkle with remaining 1/2 cup cheese; put in broiler until cheese browns. Slide ring onto a large serving plate; fill center with **Tuna and Green Beans in Mushroom Sauce, or Chicken and Peas in Celery Sauce.** Makes 6 servings.

TUNA AND GREEN BEANS IN MUSHROOM SAUCE: Combine a **10½- or 11-ounce can condensed mushroom soup, 1/2 cup milk, 2 cups cooked green beans** and a **7-ounce can tuna.** Heat to boiling.

CHICKEN AND PEAS IN CELERY SAUCE: Combine a **10½- or 11-ounce can condensed cream of celery soup, 1/2 cup milk, 2 cups cooked peas,** and **1 cup diced, cooked chicken.** Heat to boiling.

Salad Story

Once upon a time, in the ancient days of Rome, so the story goes, a well-to-do citizen found himself left alone for dinner. All he could find to eat was a dish of cold "herbs," as greens were called. Tasteless fare, indeed, he thought. He looked further and emerged with a flask of olive oil, a lemon, salt, and herbs and precious spices from the East. Mixing and tasting as he went along, he made a "sauce" that pleased him and poured it over the greens. So pleased was he that he passed the idea along to his wife, and the salad, as we know it today was born!

Modern salads are so versatile that they can take their place anywhere in the menu, from appetizer to dessert.

APPETIZER SALADS

Appetizer salads had their start in California, and we think they're a fine idea. A small serving of a green salad, such as our Caesar Salad on page 62, whets the appetite for courses that follow.

GREEN SALADS

Men prefer tossed green salads above all others, and like to make them, too! Such a salad may be served, with the main course or separately. Be sure the dressing is well-seasoned, and add it to the greens the very last minute.

There are many greens besides lettuce—don't neglect any of them. Tender, raw spinach leaves, dandelion greens, romaine, escarole, chicory, Chinese cabbage, green, red, and Savoy cabbage, French endive, water cress, turnip, mustard, and beet greens—even nasturtium leaves—combine any two, three or more.

HEARTY SALADS

Soup, salad, and dessert—a sure-to-please formula for lunch or supper, if the salad is hearty. Made with chicken, tuna, salmon, shellfish, hard-cooked eggs, ham, cheese, or other protein foods, combined, perhaps with potatoes, macaroni, or kidney beans, and served on crisp greens, such salads satisfy both eye and appetite.

DESSERT SALADS

Combine salad and dessert in a single course, with a creation like our Fruit Salad with Cottage Cheese, Frozen Fruit or Cheese Salad, all on page 72, or a Mix-Your-Own Fruit Salad, page 71.

CAESAR SALAD

6 tablespoons salad oil	1 egg
2 garlic cloves	1/4 cup wine vinegar
2 slices day-old bread, cubed	1 small can anchovy fillets
2 quarts crisp, mixed salad	1/4 cup grated Parmesan cheese
greens (lettuce, romaine,	Salt
chicory, watercress)	Pepper

Combine salad oil and garlic; let stand several hours. Remove garlic. Put 2 tablespoons of garlic-oil in a skillet. Saute bread cubes until crisp and brown. Place mixed greens in deep salad bowl. Break egg over greens. Add remaining garlic-oil, vinegar, anchovies, grated cheese, and croutons. Sprinkle with salt and pepper to taste. Toss until greens glisten with dressing and all trace of the egg has disappeared. Makes 6 to 8 servings.

RAW VEGETABLE SALAD: Combine **1 cup shredded raw carrots, 1 cup thinly sliced cauliflower, 1 cup diced celery, 3 cups shredded lettuce.** Toss with **1/2 cup French dressing.** Makes 6 servings.

RAW CAULIFLOWER SALAD: Separate **1 small head cauliflower** into flowerets; slice flowerets crosswise into thin slices. Add **1/2 cup diced green pepper.** Toss with **1/2 cup French dressing.** Serve on **shredded lettuce.** Makes 6 to 8 servings.

CHEF'S SALAD

1 head chicory	1/4 pound Swiss cheese
1 bunch watercress	6 small tomatoes
1/4 pound boiled ham	8 large stuffed olives

Wash chicory and watercress; drain. Break or cut in bite-size pieces. Put in vegetable crisper in refrigerator for 1 hour or more. Cut ham and cheese in thin strips. Slice tomatoes and olives. Put greens in salad bowl. Arrange remaining ingredients in attractive pattern on top. Just before serving, pour over Snappy French Dressing; toss. Makes 6 to 8 servings.

SNAPPY FRENCH DRESSING

1/2 cup salad oil	3/4 teaspoon dry mustard
3 tablespoons vinegar	1/2 teaspoon paprika
3/4 teaspoon salt	Dash pepper
2 teaspoons sugar	2 tablespoons minced onion

Put all ingredients in a jar with a tight-fitting cover. Let stand at least 1/2 hour. Shake before using. Makes about 3/4 cup.

GOLDEN POTATO SALAD

4 cups diced, cold boiled potatoes	1 cup chopped celery
1 small onion, chopped	1 teaspoon salt
2 tablespoons chopped parsley	Mustard Salad Dressing
	Crisp lettuce

Combine potatoes, onion, parsley, celery, and salt. Pour over Mustard Salad Dressing and stir gently till well-mixed. Let stand about 1 hour. Arrange lettuce in a salad bowl. Put potato mixture on lettuce. Garnish with sliced tomatoes and cucumbers, if desired. Makes 6 to 8 servings.

MUSTARD SALAD DRESSING

4 tablespoons yellow prepared mustard	2 tablespoons sugar
2 tablespoons light cream or evaporated milk	2 tablespoons vinegar
	1/4 teaspoon salt
	Dash pepper

Combine all ingredients; beat with a rotary beater until light and fluffy. Makes about 2/3 cup.

CHICKEN SALAD

3 cups diced cooked chicken	1 tablespoon lemon juice
1½ cups diced celery	1/2 teaspoon salt
1 cup salted peanuts	Crisp lettuce
1/2 cup mayonnaise or salad dressing	Tomato wedges
	Cucumber slices

Mix chicken, celery, and peanuts in large bowl. Blend mayonnaise, lemon juice, and salt in small bowl. Pour seasoned dressing over chicken mixture and toss. Chill. Line salad bowl with lettuce; pile chicken mixture in center. Arrange tomato wedges and cucumber slices around edge. Makes 6 servings.

HAM SALAD MOUSSE

Soften **2 envelopes unflavored gelatine** in **1/3 cup cold water;** dissolve over boiling water. Whip **1 cup whipping cream** until slightly stiffened. Add **4 cups ground cooked ham, 1/2 cup chopped celery, dash pepper, 1/4 cup drained pickle relish** and **2 tablespoons chopped parsley.** Combine with dissolved gelatine. Pour into 1½-quart mold. Chill until firm. Unmold on **salad greens.** Serve with highly seasoned **French dressing.** Makes 8 servings.

SEAFOOD SALAD

1 5-ounce can lobster, drained,
    boned, and cut in bite-size pieces
1 5-ounce can shrimps, drained
    and cleaned
1 6½-ounce can crab meat, drained,
    boned, and flaked
1 cup diced celery

1 tablespoon minced onion
1 tablespoon lemon juice
1 teaspoon salt
1/4 teaspoon pepper
Mayonnaise or
    salad dressing
Crisp lettuce

    Combine seafood, celery, onion, lemon juice, salt, pepper, and
3/4 cup mayonnaise or salad dressing in medium-size bowl. Toss to
mix well. Cover and chill thoroughly. Line salad bowl with lettuce; fill
with salad mixture; garnish with additional salad dressing. Sprinkle
with **paprika,** if desired. Makes 4 to 6 servings.

TUNA APPLE SALAD

    Drain **two 7-ounce cans tuna;** flake. Combine with **2 cups diced,
pared, tart apples, 1 cup diced celery, 2 cups shredded lettuce** and
1/2 cup broken walnuts. Add **1/2 cup mayonnaise;** toss lightly.
Arrange on **salad greens.** Makes 6 servings.

SALMON SALAD BOWL

1 7¾-ounce can salmon
Watercress or salad greens
1 large sweet onion, sliced
2 tomatoes, cut in wedges

1/2 cucumber, scored and sliced
2 carrots, made into curls
1 green pepper, cut in rings
1 cup cooked or canned peas

1 cup Blue Cheese Dressing

Drain salmon; flake, keeping pieces as large as possible. Arrange water cress in center of shallow salad bowl. Put salmon on top. Around salmon, arrange all other ingredients except dressing, which is served separately. Makes 4 servings.

CARROT CURLS: Scrape carrots and cut in paper-thin strips, lengthwise, with a vegetable scraper or sharp paring knife. Roll into curls; fasten with wooden picks. Crisp in ice water. Remove wooden picks before serving.

BLUE CHEESE DRESSING

Mash a **2-ounce package blue cheese** with a fork. Blend in **1 cup bottled creamy French Dressing.** Mix well. Makes about 1 cup.

TUNA MACARONI SALAD

4 cups chilled, cooked elbow
  macaroni (1 8-ounce package)
1 7-ounce can tuna, flaked into
  large pieces
1/2 cup chopped celery
1 small onion, finely chopped

2 tablespoons chopped pimiento
1/2 cup mayonnaise or
  salad dressing
2 teaspoons lemon juice
1/4 teaspoon Worcestershire
1½ teaspoons salt
Crisp lettuce

Combine macaroni, tuna, celery, onion, and pimiento in medium-size bowl. Blend mayonnaise, lemon juice, Worcestershire, and salt, in small bowl. Pour seasoned dressing over macaroni-tuna mixture and toss. Arrange on lettuce in a salad bowl. Makes 4 to 6 servings.

SALMON SLAW

1 1-pound can salmon
4 cups shredded cabbage

1/2 cup mayonnaise or salad dressing
Lettuce
Capers

Flake salmon in small pieces, removing bones and skin. Add to cabbage with mayonnaise; toss to mix thoroughly. Serve in lettuce cups; garnish with capers. Makes 6 servings.

COTTAGE CHEESE-VEGETABLE RING

2 envelopes unflavored gelatine
1/2 cup cold water
1 cup large-curd cottage cheese
1 cup ketchup
1 cup salad dressing or
    mayonnaise
1/2 cup whipping cream, whipped
2 tablespoons chopped parsley
2 tablespoons chopped pimiento

2 tablespoons chopped onion
1 tablespoon lemon juice
1/2 teaspoon Worcestershire
Dash Tabasco
1/2 teaspoon monosodium
    glutamate
Salt to taste
Crisp salad greens
Vegetable Salad Medley

Sprinkle gelatine on cold water; dissolve over hot water; cool slightly. Mix cottage cheese, ketchup, and salad dressing; stir in dissolved gelatine. Fold in whipped cream. Add all remaining ingredients except salad greens, blending gently but thoroughly. Turn into an oiled 5-cup ring mold; chill until firm. Unmold on a large platter. Garnish with salad greens. Fill center of ring with Vegetable Salad Medley. Makes 8 servings.

VEGETABLE SALAD MEDLEY: Drain **two 16-ounce cans mixed vegetables or** cook, drain, and cool **two 12-ounce packages frozen mixed vegetables.** Combine **1/2 cup salad oil, 2 tablespoons vinegar, 1/2 teaspoon garlic salt, dash Tabasco,** and **1/4 teaspoon paprika.** Beat with rotary beater. Pour over vegetables. Chill.

MOLDED SPRING VEGETABLE SALAD

1 package lemon flavored gelatin
2 cups water
1 teaspoon salt
1 teaspoon vinegar

1 cup sliced radishes
1 cup diced cucumber
1/2 cup sliced green onions
Crisp salad greens

Mayonnaise

Dissolve gelatin in water as directed on package. Add salt and vinegar. Chill until consistency of unbeaten egg white. Arrange a few radish slices in bottom of an oiled 5-cup ring mold. Pour in a little gelatin to "anchor" radishes. Chill till set. Fold remaining radishes, cucumber, and onions in remaining gelatin. Pour into mold. Chill until set. Unmold on a large serving platter. Garnish with salad greens. Serve with mayonnaise. Makes 8 servings.

JELLIED VEGETABLE SALAD: Soften **2 tablespoons unflavored gelatine** in **1/4 cup cold water**; dissolve in **1 cup boiling water**. Add **1/4 cup sugar, 1 teaspoon salt, 2 tablespoons lemon juice** and **1/4 cup vinegar.** Chill until syrupy. Combine **1/2 cup each grated raw carrots, chopped celery,** and **shredded cabbage**; fold in with **1 cup cooked or canned peas.** Pour into 6 to 8 individual molds; chill till firm. Serve on **crisp salad greens** with **mayonnaise.**

WALDORF SALAD

2 cups diced unpared red   1/2 cup mayonnaise or
    apples   salad dressing
1 cup diced celery   1/2 cup coarsely chopped walnuts
           Chicory or other salad greens

Combine apples, celery, and mayonnaise; chill. Just before serving, fold in nuts; spoon on to salad plates; garnish with chicory. Makes 4 servings.

MIX-YOUR-OWN FRUIT SALAD: Arrange fresh fruits attractively on a large platter. For example: **melon balls** (watermelon, honeydew, and cantaloupe); **pineapple chunks,** fresh, canned, or frozen; **fluted banana slices; orange** and **grapefruit sections.** Keep the fruits separate for easy selection. Serve **mixed salad greens** and **Fruit Salad Dressing** in separate bowls.

FRUIT SALAD DRESSING: Combine **2 tablespoons flour** and **2/3 cup sugar.** Beat **2 eggs** till light. Stir into flour mixture. Strain **juice of 1 lemon** and **juice of 1 orange.** Add to **1 cup pineapple juice.** Stir into egg mixture. Cook over hot water, until thickened, stirring constantly. Chill. Whip **1 cup whipping cream.** Fold into cooked mixture. Makes about 3 cups.

71

FRUIT SALAD WITH COTTAGE CHEESE

1 pound creamy cottage
   cheese
1/4 cup strained honey
Crisp lettuce
2 bananas, peeled and sliced
1½ cups pineapple chunks
2 cups melon balls

1 cup grapefruit sections
1 cup orange sections
1 cup blueberries, strawberries,
   or raspberries
Fresh mint
1/2 cup mayonnaise or
   salad dressing
1/2 cup sour cream

Combine cheese and honey. Arrange lettuce in shallow bowl. Pile cheese on lettuce in a mound. Mix fruits together lightly and arrange around cheese. Garnish with mint. Combine mayonnaise and sour cream; serve separately. Makes 6 to 8 servings.

FROZEN FRUIT SALAD: Whip **1 cup whipping cream;** fold in **1 cup mayonnaise, 1 cup diced orange sections** and **1 cup pineapple tidbits.** Spoon into refrigerator freezing tray. Freeze, without stirring, with cold control at lowest setting. Cut into squares. Serve on **water cress** with **French dressing.** Makes 6 to 8 servings.

FROZEN CHEESE SALAD: Mash **two 3-ounce packages cream cheese.** Add **1/4 cup each chopped stuffed olives** and **chopped toasted almonds, 1/4 teaspoon salt, 2 teaspoons lemon juice.** Whip **1/4 cup whipping cream;** fold in. Freeze and serve as for Frozen Fruit Salad above.

A Loaf of Bread---

Never mind the wine, Omar Khayam or no! A warm, crisply brown loaf, cooling on a rack, is all we ask. We've had the fun of mixing and kneading and watching the dough rise. We've sniffed the heavenly scent of making bread, and now, with knife poised, we are ready for the treat of treats, the crust, sliced warm from the loaf, butter melting as it touches the velvety crumb. Then we can wait for the rest of the loaf to cool before slicing.

If you've never baked with yeast, there's fun in store for you. Never believe that it is difficult, or that the knack is hard to acquire. Just use a tested recipe, be sure the yeast is fresh (dry, active yeast is dated on the package), the flour of good quality, and go ahead.

You'll soon learn to judge the temperature of yeast mixtures and to know the feel of the dough as it kneads into a smooth, elastic ball under the heels of your hands. Then you are all set to surprise the family with rolls, buns, and coffee cakes of your own devising.

Don't forget the hot-roll mixes that are on your grocer's shelf. These make fine rolls and bread, and, with a few extra touches, fancy sweet rolls, rings, and braids.

Quick breads—biscuits, muffins, griddlecakes, waffles, and doughnuts are all favorites in American homes. There are mixes for biscuits, capable of wide variaton, from coffee cake to pancakes, and there are special mixes for muffins, waffles, pancakes, and even doughnuts.

And when you're in the mood to get out the mixing bowl and begin at the beginning, you'll love our tested recipes for such unusual breads as buttermilk griddlecakes, banana doughnuts, dessert waffles, sultana rolls, and others.

There are a few tricks in making quick breads that are important to remember:

1. When adding liquid ingredients to dry, stir only enough to dampen the latter. Overstirring or beating causes ugly tunnels to form inside the loaf or muffin and makes for uneven rising, so that the loaf or muffin is lop-sided or peaked.

2. If waffles stick, either the waffle baker was too cold at the start, or there wasn't enough shortening in the recipe.

3. Put greased muffin pans in the oven and let them get sizzling hot before spooning in the batter—you'll get bigger muffins.

Now go ahead and try a recipe. Have fun!

WHITE BREAD

1 cup milk	1 package active dry yeast
3 tablespoons sugar	1 cup warm (not hot) water
2½ teaspoons salt	6 cups sifted flour
6 tablespoons shortening	Melted shortening

Scald milk; stir in sugar, salt, and shortening; stir until sugar dissolves; cool to lukewarm. Sprinkle yeast on water; stir till dissolved. Add milk mixture. Stir in 3 cups of the flour; beat till smooth. Stir in remaining flour. Turn out on a lightly floured board. Knead: Fold dough over toward you. Press down away from you with the heel of your hand. Give dough a quarter turn. Continue until dough is smooth and elastic, and does not stick to the board. Place in a greased bowl; brush top of dough with melted shortening. Cover with a damp cloth; let rise in warm place, 80°F. to 85°F., until doubled in bulk, about 1 hour.

Punch down; turn out on lightly floured board. Divide dough. Shape into 2 loaves; place in greased loaf pans, 9 x 5 x 3 inches. Cover with a damp cloth; let rise in a warm place, 80°F. to 85°F., until center of dough is slightly higher than the edges of the pans, about 1 hour.

Set oven for hot, 400°F. Bake 50 minutes to 1 hour. Remove from pans immediately and cool on a rack. Makes 2 loaves bread.

PARKER HOUSE ROLLS
(see picture, page 74)

Prepare **dough** using recipe for White Bread (see p. 74.) Divide the dough. Roll out 1/2 inch thick, on a lightly floured board. Cut with a 2½-inch round cutter. Crease heavily across center with the dull edge of a knife. Brush lightly with **melted shortening.** Fold over. Place on a greased baking sheet about 1 inch apart. Cover with a damp cloth. Let rest in a warm place, 80°F. to 85°F., until double in bulk.

Set oven for hot, 400°F. Bake rolls 20 minutes or until brown. Remove from pan immediately. Makes 2 dozen rolls.

Many fancy rolls can be made from bread dough. Here are a few:

BOWKNOTS: Roll pieces of dough in "ropes" 6 to 8 inches long and 1/2 inch in diameter. Tie loosely in bowknots.

CLOVERLEAF ROLLS: Shape dough into small balls about 3/4 inch in diameter; place 3 balls in each section of greased muffin pans.

CARAWAY CRESCENTS: Roll 1/4 of dough in circle 9 inches in diameter and 1/4 inch thick. Cut into 12 wedge-shaped pieces. Roll up each wedge starting at round edge. Place on greased baking sheet with pointed end under; shape like crescents; brush with **melted butter or margarine;** sprinkle with **caraway seeds.**

POPPY SEED BRAIDS: Roll pieces of dough in thin ropes 12 to 14 inches long and 1/4 inch in diameter. Braid 3 ropes together; cut off in desired lengths; pinch ends together firmly. Brush with **melted butter or margarine;** sprinkle with **poppy seeds.**

CINNAMON NUT TWISTS: Roll pieces of dough in ropes 7 inches long and 1/4 inch in diameter. Dip in **melted butter,** then in a mixture of **sugar, cinnamon, chopped nuts.** Form in figure 8's.

ALMOND TWISTS
(see picture upper left p. 78)

Prepare recipe for **Swedish Coffee Cake** (p. 78). Combine **1 cup blanched and shredded almonds** with **2/3 cup sugar;** drop the dough by spoonfuls into the sugar-nut mixture and toss lightly until each portion is well coated: shape each roll into a rope about 6 inches long. Twist into figure 8's. Place on well-greased baking sheet; let stand 5 minutes; bake in moderate oven, 375°F., for 25 to 30 minutes. Makes about 8 to 10 twists.

PECAN BUNS

1¼ cups milk	3/4 cup sugar
1 package active dry yeast	2 eggs
1/4 cup warm water	1/2 cup brown sugar
5 cups sifted flour	1 tablespoon cinnamon
1½ teaspoons salt	1/2 cup chopped pecans
1 tablespoon sugar	3/4 cup raisins
3/4 cup butter or margarine	1 cup light corn syrup

Scald milk; cool to lukewarm. Dissolve yeast in water. Combine milk and yeast. Add 2 cups flour, salt, and the 1 tablespoon sugar; beat till smooth. Set in warm place until bubbly. Cream 1/2 cup butter and 3/4 cup sugar till fluffy. Add eggs, one at a time; beat well. Add yeast mixture. Beat till smooth. Stir in remaining flour. Knead till smooth and elastic. (See recipe for Bread p. 74.) Cover; let rise in warm place till double in bulk. Divide dough in half. Roll out on floured board into rectangles about 1/4 inch thick. Spread with remaining 1/4 cup butter; sprinkle with brown sugar, cinnamon, chopped nuts, and raisins. Roll up like jelly roll; cut in 2-inch slices. Grease muffin pans; put a **few whole pecans** in each cup, add syrup about 1/4 inch deep. Place slices in cups, cut side up. Cover; let stand till double in bulk. Bake in moderate oven, 350°F., about 35 minutes, or till brown. Turn out of pans at once. Makes about 24 buns.

HOT CROSS BUNS

1 cup milk	5 cups sifted flour
1/3 cup butter or margarine	(about)
1/2 cup sugar	2 eggs, beaten
1½ teaspoons salt	1 cup golden raisins
2 packages active dry yeast	Melted shortening
1/4 cup warm water	Confectioners' Sugar Icing

Scald milk; add butter, sugar, and salt. Stir till sugar dissolves; cool to lukewarm. Sprinkle yeast on water; stir till dissolved. Add to milk mixture. Add half the flour; mix well. Stir in eggs. Add enough flour to make a soft dough; mix well. Knead about 10 minutes. (See recipe for Bread, p. 74.) Place in a greased bowl; brush with shortening. Cover; let rise in warm place till double in bulk, about 2 hours. Punch down. Turn out on floured board; knead in raisins. Shape into 1½-inch balls. Place in greased pans, 1 inch apart. Brush with **egg yolk** diluted with a little **water**. Cover; let rise till double in bulk, about 1 hour. Bake in moderately hot oven, 375°F., 30 minutes. Cool. Make crosses on buns with Confectioners' Sugar Icing. Makes about 2½ dozen buns.

CONFECTIONERS' SUGAR ICING: Mix together **1 cup sifted confectioners' sugar, 1½ tablespoons warm milk**, a **little vanilla**.

77

SWEDISH COFFEE RING

1/2 cup plus 2 tablespoons milk	3 to 3½ cups sifted flour
1/2 cup shortening	2 eggs, beaten
1/2 cup sugar	Melted shortening
1/2 teaspoon salt	Melted butter
1 package active dry yeast	2/3 cup brown sugar
2 tablespoons lukewarm water	2 teaspoons cinnamon

Scald milk. Add shortening, sugar, and salt. Stir till sugar dissolves; cool to lukewarm. Dissolve yeast in water; combine with milk mixture. Stir in 1½ cups flour; add eggs; beat well. Add enough flour to make a soft dough. Turn out on lightly floured board; knead till smooth and elastic. (See recipe for Bread, p. 74.) Put in a greased bowl; brush with shortening; cover and let rise in a warm place, 80°F. to 85°F., till double in bulk, about 2 hours. Turn out on floured board; roll into a rectangle about 8 x 12 inches. Brush with butter. Sprinkle with brown sugar and cinnamon. Roll up like a jelly roll; shape into a ring on greased baking sheet; seal ends. From the outside cut through the ring toward center almost all the way through, in 1 inch slices. Turn slices slightly on side. Brush with shortening; cover; let rise about 45 minutes or till double in bulk. Bake in moderately hot oven, 375°F., 25 to 30 minutes. While warm spread with Confectioners' Sugar Icing (see p. 77); sprinkle with **chopped nuts**. Makes 1 ring.

Recipe for Almond Twists (upper left), page 75

Recipe for Glazed Spicy Raisin Biscuits (upper right), page 80; Quick Coffee Cake (lower left), page 80

BAKING POWDER BISCUITS
(upper left)

2½ cups sifted flour **1/2 teaspoon salt**
4 teaspoons baking powder **1/3 cup shortening**
3/4 cup milk (about)

Set oven for very hot, 450°F. Sift together first 3 ingredients. Cut in shortening with 2 knives or a pastry blender. Add enough milk to make soft dough. Pat out 1/2 inch thick on lightly floured board. Cut with 2-inch biscuit cutter. Place on baking sheet. Bake till brown, 12 to 15 minutes. Makes about 16 biscuits.

SULTANA ROLLS
(lower right)

Recipe Baking Powder Biscuits **1/2 cup brown sugar,**
2 tablespoons melted butter or **firmly packed**
margarine **1 teaspoon cinnamon**
1/4 cup seedless raisins

Set oven for hot, 425°F. Grease a baking pan, 9 x 13 inches. Prepare dough as directed above in Baking Powder Biscuits. Roll out on a lightly floured board, in a rectangle about 8 x 16 inches. Brush with butter. Combine remaining ingredients. Sprinkle over dough. Roll up firmly, like a jelly-roll, starting at wide side. Seal edge. Cut in 1-inch slices. Place, cut side up, in pan. Bake 15 to 18 minutes, or till brown. Makes about 16 rolls.

GLAZED SPICY RAISIN BISCUITS
(upper right, page 79)

2½ cups sifted flour	1/3 cup shortening
4 teaspoons baking powder	1 egg, well-beaten
1/2 teaspoon salt	Milk
1/4 teaspoon cinnamon	1/2 cup seedless raisins
1/4 teaspoon nutmeg	2 tablespoons sugar
2 tablespoons sugar	2 tablespoons whipping cream

Set oven for very hot, 450°F. Grease a baking sheet. Sift together first 6 ingredients. Cut in shortening with 2 knives or a pastry blender. Put egg in a measuring cup; add milk to make 3/4 cup. Stir into flour mixture. Stir in raisins. Pat out on a lightly floured board 1/2 inch thick. Cut with biscuit cutter. Place on baking sheet; bake 10 to 12 minutes, or till light brown. Whip cream with a fork; stir in remaining sugar. Brush over biscuits. Brown in broiler 2 to 3 minutes. Makes about 2 dozen 1½-inch biscuits.

Note: If you like tall, fluffy baking powder biscuits, don't knead the dough, roll it 1/2- to 3/4-inch thick and set the biscuits close together in the pan. For firmer texture and crisper crust, knead the dough for a few minutes before rolling out, cut 3/8- to 1/2-inch thick and set the biscuits farther apart in the pan.

QUICK COFFEE CAKE
(lower left, page 79)

1⅓ cups biscuit mix	2/3 cup milk
3/4 cup sugar	3 tablespoons melted butter
3 tablespoons shortening,	or margarine
softened	1/3 cup brown sugar, firmly packed
1 egg, well-beaten	2 tablespoons cream
1 teaspoon vanilla	1/3 cup slivered, blanched almonds

Set oven for moderate, 350°F. Grease an 8-inch square pan. Combine biscuit mix and sugar. Add shortening, egg, vanilla, and 1/3 cup milk. Beat 1 minute. Gradually add remaining 1/3 cup milk. Turn into pan. Bake about 30 minutes, or till light brown. Meanwhile mix butter, brown sugar, cream, and almonds. Spread over baked cake. Put in broiler 3 inches from heat 3 to 5 minutes or till topping browns. Cut in squares. Makes 12 to 16 servings.

BLUEBERRY MUFFINS

1/4 cup shortening	4 teaspoons baking powder
1/3 cup sugar	3/4 teaspoon salt
2 eggs, well-beaten	2/3 cup milk
2 cups sifted flour	2/3 cup blueberries

Set oven for hot, 400°F.

Beat shortening until creamy; add sugar gradually, continuing to beat. Stir in eggs. Sift together 1⅔ cups of the flour, baking powder, and salt. Add alternately with milk to egg mixture. Stir just enough to blend. Mix blueberries with remaining 1/3 cup flour; stir in lightly. Pour into greased muffin pans. Bake 30 minutes or till brown. Makes about 14 muffins.

ZANTE MUFFINS: Cream **1/3 cup shortening** and **1 cup sugar** until light and fluffy. Beat **2 eggs** until thick and lemon-colored; stir into sugar mixture with **1¼ cups yellow cornmeal.** Mix and sift **3/4 cup sifted flour, 2½ teaspoons baking powder** and **3/4 teaspoon salt;** stir in **1/3 cup dried currants** or **1/2 cup broken walnut meats;** combine with cornmeal mixture. Stir in **1 cup milk,** mixing just enough to moisten dry ingredients. Spoon into greased muffin pans. Bake in hot oven, 400°F., about 25 minutes, or until brown. Makes 12 large or 18 medium-size muffins.

CRISP WAFFLES

2 cups sifted cake flour	2 egg yolks
3 teaspoons baking powder	1¼ cups milk
1/4 teaspoon salt	1/3 cup melted shortening
2 egg whites	

Heat waffle iron according to manufacturer's directions. Sift together flour, baking powder, and salt. Beat egg yolks until light. Combine with milk; add to eggs. Add milk mixture slowly to dry ingredients, stirring until batter is smooth. Add shortening. Whip egg whites till stiff, but not dry; fold into flour mixture. Bake in heated waffle iron. Serve with **hot syrup** and **butter.** Makes 6 to 8 waffles.

DESSERT WAFFLES: Stir **1/2 cup chopped nuts** into batter. Serve with **chocolate sauce** and **whipped cream.**

APPLE WAFFLES: Add **1/4 teaspoon cinnamon** to dry ingredients; fold **1½ cups chopped tart apples** into batter. Serve with **sausages.**

BLUEBERRY WAFFLES: Combine **1 cup fresh blueberries** and **2 tablespoons sugar**; fold into batter. Or, add 2 cups frozen blueberries, drained and thawed.

ORANGE WAFFLES: Decrease milk to 3/4 cup. Add **1/2 cup orange juice** and **2 teaspoons grated orange rind** to batter.

BUTTERMILK GRIDDLECAKES

2 cups sifted flour   1 tablespoon sugar
1 teaspoon baking soda   2 eggs, well-beaten
1/2 teaspoon salt   2 cups buttermilk
2 tablespoons melted shortening

Sift together flour, baking soda, salt, and sugar. Combine eggs and buttermilk; stir into flour mixture; beat until smooth; add shortening. Bake on hot griddle. Serve with butter and maple syrup. Makes about 18 griddlecakes.

SAUSAGE GRIDDLECAKES: Fold **1/2 cup cooked sausage meat** into batter prepared according to directions above.

BANANA-WALNUT GRIDDLECAKES: Slice **1 large banana** very thin; fold into batter with **1/3 cup chopped walnuts.**

CORN GRIDDLECAKES: Add **1 cup drained canned or cooked corn** to liquid ingredients.

CLAM GRIDDLECAKES: Drain **1 can minced clams.** Reserve liquor. Omit sugar; increase **melted shortening** to 1/4 cup. Substitute liquor for part of the buttermilk. Fold clams into batter with **1 teaspoon grated onion or 1 tablespoon finely cut chives.** Serve with **ketchup or tomato sauce.**

BANANA DOUGHNUTS

5 cups sifted flour	1 cup sugar
4 teaspoons baking powder	3 eggs, well-beaten
1 teaspoon baking soda	3/4 cup mashed ripe bananas
2 teaspoons salt	1/2 cup sour milk or buttermilk
1 teaspoon nutmeg	1½ teaspoons vanilla
1/4 cup shortening	1/2 cup flour for rolling

Melted fat or salad oil

Sift together flour, baking powder, soda, salt, and nutmeg. Beat shortening until creamy. Add sugar gradually and continue beating until light and fluffy. Add eggs and beat well. Add bananas, milk, and vanilla to sugar mixture and blend. Add dry ingredients and mix until smooth. Turn a small amount of dough onto a floured board. Knead very lightly. Roll out 3/8- or 1/2-inch thick. Cut with floured 2½-inch doughnut cutter.

Heat fat or salad oil in a heavy kettle or deep fat-fryer. Have fat 3 to 4 inches deep. Heat to 375°F. on a deep fat thermometer, or until a 1-inch cube of bread browns in about 40 seconds. Slip doughnuts into fat with spatula. Fry about 3 minutes, or until golden brown, turning frequently. Drain on absorbent paper. If desired, sprinkle with **granulated or powdered sugar,** or a mixture of **sugar and cinnamon.** Makes about 3½ dozen doughnuts.

Let's Bake a Cake

There are wonderful cake mixes on the market—mixes that make light-as-a-feather angel food and "butter" cakes of several types. But, if you are like us, once in awhile you like to start from scratch, and make a really special cake, just to prove your hand hasn't lost its skill! Or, you want to make a cake that's a family favorite, like old-fashioned applesauce loaf cake, or an airy sponge cake, for which no mix is available.

SHARING SECRETS

Every baker of good cakes has a few secrets. We have, too, and we're going to share them with you.

The first thing you need is a tried and true recipe, because a good cake is never a hit-or-miss affair. The finest of ingredients must go into its making—cake flour or a reliable enriched flour, depending on the recipe—farm-fresh eggs, and high quality shortening, and so on. Have **all** ingredients at room temperature.

Great-grandmother may have used a tea-cup or coffee-cup for measuring, but remember, she always used the same cup. Today there is no excuse for haphazard measurements. Standardized measuring cups and spoons are available today everywhere at small cost.

However the way you **use** these measures is important:

1. Always sift flour before measuring. Then spoon gently into the cup, and level it off with a spatula. Sift **again** with baking powder and salt.

2. Dip a measuring spoon into **dry ingredients** called for, then level off with a spatula.

3. Press **brown sugar** firmly into the cup when measuring.

4. Nested cups are helpful in measuring fractions of cupfuls.

5. Press **shortening** firmly into the measure, being careful not to leave air spaces, and level off. Or use the water-displacement method. For example, to measure 1/2 cup shortening, fill cup 1/2 full of cold water; add shortening until water rises to 1-cup level; then drain off all water.

6. To measure **liquids,** set the cup on a level surface and pour in the liquid until it reaches the correct graduation mark. A cup with the 1-cup mark **below** the rim is best for measuring liquids.

7. Measure all ingredients and set the oven for correct temperature before you begin to mix.

8. Use the size of pan recommended in the recipe. And follow directions for oven temperature and baking time.

These are our most important secrets. Our best recipes follow.

SILVER CAKE

1½ cups sifted cake flour	1/2 cup milk
2 teaspoons baking powder	1/2 teaspoon almond flavoring
Few grains salt	1/2 teaspoon vanilla
1/3 cup shortening	3 egg whites
3/4 cup sugar	Satiny Chocolate Frosting
	1 cup chopped nuts

Set oven for moderately hot, 375°F. Grease and flour two 8-inch round cake pans. Sift together flour, baking powder, and salt. Cream shortening and sugar until fluffy. Combine milk and flavorings. Add alternately with flour mixture to sugar mixture. Whip egg whites till stiff; fold into flour mixture. Spoon into pans. Bake 25 to 30 minutes, or till brown. Cool in pans 5 minutes. Remove and cool on racks. Fill and frost with Satiny Chocolate Frosting. Cover sides with nuts. Makes one 2-layer 8-inch cake.

SATINY CHOCOLATE FROSTING: Mix together **6 tablespoons flour** and **6 tablespoons sugar;** slowly add **2 cups milk.** Stir until smooth. Cook over low heat until thick, stirring constantly. Add **1 cup butter or margarine, 1 teaspoon vanilla,** and **2 squares melted unsweetened chocolate.** Stir well. Cool. Makes enough to fill and frost one 2-layer 8- or 9-inch cake.

LORD BALTIMORE CAKE

Bake 2 layers of white or yellow cake using your favorite recipe, or packaged cake mix. Cool thoroughly. Follow directions below for frosting and filling.

1⅔ cups sugar	Few drops red food coloring
1/2 cup water	1/4 cup fine dry macaroon crumbs
1/3 cup light corn syrup	1/4 cup chopped walnuts
2 egg whites	8 Maraschino cherries, chopped
1/4 teaspoon salt	8 whole Maraschino cherries
1 teaspoon vanilla	1/3 cup chopped walnuts

Combine sugar, water, and corn syrup in saucepan; stir over low heat until sugar dissolves; bring to boiling. Cover; boil 2 to 3 minutes. Remove cover; boil without stirring to 240°F. on a candy thermometer, or soft ball stage. Wipe any crystals from saucepan with dampened cheesecloth during cooking. Remove from heat. Whip egg whites until foamy; add salt; whip stiff. Pour syrup on eggs in fine stream, beating steadily. Continue beating until frosting stands in peaks. Add vanilla. Tint pink with red coloring. Put 1/3 of frosting in a small bowl; stir in next 3 ingredients. Spread on a cake layer. Top with second layer. Spread remaining frosting on top and sides of cake. Garnish with whole cherries and remaining nuts. Makes 1 cake.

CHOCOLATE CAKE

2 cups sifted cake flour	2 eggs
2 teaspoons baking powder	1 teaspoon vanilla
1/2 teaspoon baking soda	4 squares unsweetened
1/2 teaspoon salt	chocolate, melted
1/2 cup shortening	1 cup plus 2 tablespoons milk
2 cups brown sugar, firmly packed	Coffee Frosting

Set oven for moderate, 350°F. Grease and flour two 8-inch round cake pans. Sift together flour, baking powder, baking soda, and salt. Cream shortening; add sugar gradually; beat until fluffy. Add eggs, one at a time; beat well after each addition; stir in vanilla and chocolate. Add dry ingredients alternately with milk; stir only enough to blend well. Pour into pans. Bake 30 minutes or till cake springs back when pressed with fingertip. Cool in pans 5 minutes. Remove; cool on a rack. Fill and frost with Coffee Frosting. Garnish with chocolate sprinkles, if desired.

COFFEE FROSTING: Combine **2 egg whites, 1½ cups sugar, 1/2 teaspoon cream of tartar, 1/3 cup strong coffee** and **2 teaspoons light corn syrup** in top of a double boiler; stir to blend well. Place over boiling water and beat with a rotary beater until frosting holds its shape. Remove from heat; continue beating until frosting stands in peaks.

SPANISH CAKE

1¾ cups sifted cake flour
2 teaspoons baking powder
1/2 teaspoon salt
1 teaspoon cinnamon

1/2 cup shortening
1 cup sugar
2 eggs, well-beaten
1 teaspoon vanilla

1/2 cup milk

Set oven for moderately hot, 375°F. Grease and flour two 8-inch round cake pans. Sift together first 4 ingredients. Cream shortening till soft. Add sugar gradually, continuing to beat. Add eggs, and vanilla; beat well. Add dry ingredients to egg mixture alternately with milk. Beat only enough to blend well. Pour into pans. Bake 25 to 30 minutes or till brown. Cool in pans 5 minutes. Remove and cool on a rack. Frost with **Brown Sugar Frosting.** Sprinkle with grated chocolate, if desired. Makes 1 cake.

BROWN SUGAR FROSTING: Put **1 cup granulated sugar, 1 cup firmly packed brown sugar, 2 unbeaten egg whites** and **6 tablespoons water** in the top of a double boiler. Cook over boiling water 7 minutes, beating constantly with a rotary beater. If frosting does not hold its shape, continue cooking and beating a minute or two longer. Remove from heat; stir in **2 teaspoons vanilla.** Spread between layers and on outside of cake.

MARBLE CAKE

1¾ cups sifted cake flour	1 cup sugar
2 teaspoons baking powder	2 eggs, well-beaten
1/2 teaspoon salt	1 teaspoon vanilla
1 square unsweetened chocolate	1/2 cup milk
1/2 cup shortening	2 tablespoons milk

Set oven for moderate, 350°F. Grease and flour an 8-inch square cake pan. Sift together flour, baking powder, and salt. Melt chocolate over hot water. Cream shortening; add sugar slowly; beat until light and fluffy. Add eggs and vanilla; beat well. Add dry ingredients alternately with the 1/2 cup milk to egg mixture. Divide batter in 2 parts. Combine chocolate and remaining milk. Stir into one part; blend well. Drop alternate spoonsful of light and dark batters into cake pan. Bake 50 to 60 minutes. Cool in pan 5 minutes. Remove; cool on a rack. Frost with any favorite chocolate frosting. Makes one 8-inch square cake.

BANANA CHOCOLATE CREAM CAKE (front cover). Bake **2 cake layers.** (See Silver Cake, p. 86.) Cool. Whip **1/2 cup whipping cream;** fold in **2 tablespoons chocolate syrup.** Spread on 1 cake layer. Cover with a layer of **sliced bananas.** Top with second cake layer. Frost with any favorite **chocolate frosting.**

APPLE SAUCE CAKE

1¾ cups sifted flour	1/2 teaspoon salt
1½ teaspoons cinnamon	1 teaspoon baking soda
1 teaspoon allspice	1/2 cup shortening
1 teaspoon nutmeg	1 cup sugar
1/4 teaspoon cloves	1 egg, well-beaten

1 cup unsweetened apple sauce

Set oven for moderate, 350°F. Grease and flour a loaf pan, 9 x 5 x 3 inches.

Sift together flour, spices, salt, and baking soda. Cream shortening. Add sugar gradually; continue beating until light and fluffy. Add egg and beat well. Stir in apple sauce. Add sifted dry ingredients; stir only enough to blend. Pour into pan. Bake 50 to 60 minutes or until cake springs back when lightly touched with fingertip. Cool in pan 5 minutes. Remove and cool on a rack. Frost with **Butter Frosting**. Makes 1 cake.

BUTTER FROSTING: Blend together **2 cups sifted confectioners' sugar,** and **1/4 cup butter or margarine.** Gradually add about **2 tablespoons cream.** Stir until smooth. Add **1/2 teaspoon vanilla, 1/2 teaspoon orange flavoring,** and a **few drops each yellow and red food coloring,** if desired. Mix to blend well.

ANGEL FOOD CAKE

1 cup sifted cake flour	1 teaspoon cream of tartar
1 cup egg whites	1¼ cups sugar
1/4 teaspoon salt	1 teaspoon vanilla

Set oven for moderately low, 325°F.

Sift flour 4 times. Whip egg whites until frothy; add salt and cream of tartar; whip until stiff but not dry. Sift 2 tablespoons sugar over egg white mixture; fold in. Continue until sugar is all added. Fold in vanilla. Sift small amount flour over mixture; fold in gently. Continue until all flour is added. Pour into an ungreased 9-inch tube pan. Bake 1 hour and 15 minutes or until top springs back when touched with fingertip. Invert pan; let cake hang till cold. Loosen from sides and tube with a spatula. Frost, if desired, with **Pastel Plum Frosting,** or sprinkle with confectioners' sugar. Makes 1 cake.

PASTEL PLUM FROSTING: Combine **1/3 cup plum jelly, 1 egg white,** and **few grains salt** in the top of a double boiler. Whip with an electric mixer or rotary beater until mixed. Set over boiling water and beat constantly 3 minutes or until frosting stands in peaks. Cool. Spread on cake.

Note: Any tart jelly, such as currant or grape can be used.

SYRUP SPONGE CAKE

1 cup sifted cake flour	1¼ cups sugar
1/4 teaspoon salt	1 cup water
1 teaspoon cream of tartar	6 eggs, separated

1 teaspoon vanilla

Set oven for moderately low, 325°F.

Sift together flour, salt, and cream of tartar.

Combine sugar and water in a saucepan; stir over low heat until sugar dissolves. Cover; boil 2 minutes. Remove cover; boil without stirring to 230°F. on a candy thermometer, or till a little syrup forms a very soft ball when dropped in cold water. Whip egg whites till stiff but not dry. Pour syrup in a very thin stream on egg whites beating constantly. Continue to beat until cool.

Beat egg yolks until thick and lemon colored; fold into egg whites until thoroughly blended. Add vanilla. Sift a small amount of the flour mixture at a time over egg mixture; fold in carefully. Continue until all flour has been added. Turn into an ungreased 10-inch tube pan. Bake 1 hour or until top springs back when lightly touched with fingertip. Invert pan; let cake hang till cold. Loosen from sides and tube with a spatula. Frost, if desired with your favorite frosting or sprinkle with confectioners' sugar. Makes 1 cake.

BANANA CHIFFON CAKE

2¼ cups sifted cake flour	5 medium egg yolks, unbeaten
1½ cups sugar	1 cup mashed ripe bananas
3 teaspoons baking powder	1 tablespoon lemon juice
1 teaspoon salt	1/2 teaspoon cream of tartar
1/2 cup cooking or salad oil	1 cup egg whites

Set oven for moderately low, 325°F. Sift together flour, sugar, baking powder, and salt. Make a "well" in dry ingredients and add next 4 ingredients in order listed. Beat until smooth. Add cream of tartar to egg whites. Whip egg whites in a large mixing bowl till they form very stiff peaks. Gradually and gently fold flour mixture into egg whites, just until blended. Do not stir. Pour into an ungreased, 10-inch tube pan. Bake 1 hour 5 minutes, or until top springs back when touched with fingertip. Invert pan; let cake hang till cold. To remove, loosen from sides and tube of pan with spatula. Frost with **whipped cream** or **Banana Butter Frosting** and garnish with **banana slices** and **walnuts.** Makes 1 cake.

BANANA BUTTER FROSTING: Combine **1/2 cup mashed ripe bananas** and **1/2 teaspoon lemon juice.** Beat **1/4 cup butter or margarine** till creamy. Add **3½ cups sifted confectioners' sugar** and bananas alternately, a little at a time. Beat till light and fluffy.

Pie-The All American Favorite

In Chaucer's time, pie was considered the real test of a good cook—as he mentions in his CANTERBURY TALES. But pies in those days were massive affairs, and we doubt if the pastry would meet today's standards of flaky, golden-brown crispness!

If you hesitate to try your hand at pastry making, there is packaged pie crust mix available. Follow directions, use a light touch in mixing, and you'll have excellent results.

When you make your own pastry, there are a few rules to remember: Sift the flour before measuring. Have the water icy cold. For shortening, you can use modern, packaged lard, half lard and half butter or margarine, blended shortening which is part lard and part vegetable fat, creamy white vegetable shortening, or salad or cooking oil, which requires a special recipe (see page 104).

Now for the mixing. Use a pastry blender or two knives to cut the shortening into the flour. Pour a few drops of water into the center of the flour-shortening mixture and blend in with a fork. Continue until pastry gathers around the fork in a soft ball, leaving the inside of the bowl clean. Handle with a light, deft touch—a heavy hand and too much liquid make for tough pastry.

A canvas square on the pastry board and a stockinette cover for the rolling pin make it easier to roll out the pastry. Flour rubbed into the cloth prevents sticking or try a sheet of waxed paper thumb-tacked to the board, and **lightly** dusted with flour.

Use short, light, quick strokes with the rolling pin. Gently does it. Make a circle 1 inch larger in diameter than the pie pan. Lay the pastry gently in the pan and let it "relax" while you roll out the top crust or make the filling. Then press gently into the pan and trim off any uneven edges with scissors.

TRICKS OF THE TRADE

1. To place pastry in the pan or over filling, roll it over the rolling pin, hold it over the pie pan and unroll into place.

2. To keep a pie shell from shrinking, "hook" the bottom of each fluting under the rim of the pan. If the shell is to be baked without filling, prick the entire surface with tines of a fork.

3. To keep fruit pies from bubbling over, insert a piece or two of uncooked macaroni in the top, to act as "chimneys" to catch the juice.

Our tested recipes range from old favorites like apple and pumpkin to exotic strawberry custard and rich pecan pie. Try them all!

PUMPKIN PIE

1/2 cup sugar
1 tablespoon flour
1/2 teaspoon salt
1 teaspoon ginger
3/4 teaspoon cinnamon
1/8 teaspoon cloves
1/8 teaspoon nutmeg

1¼ cups canned pumpkin
1 tablespoon molasses
1 tablespoon melted butter or
    margarine
2 eggs, slightly beaten
1¼ cups milk
Unbaked 9-inch pie shell

Set oven for hot, 425°F. Mix sugar, flour, salt, and spices together in a large bowl. Add next five ingredients and blend thoroughly. Pour into pie shell. Bake 40 minutes or until a knife inserted near rim comes out clean. Makes 1 pie.

PUMPKIN PECAN PIE

Blend together **1 tablespoon butter or margarine, 2 tablespoons brown sugar, 1 tablespoon grated orange peel** and **3/4 cup whole pecans.** About 10 minutes before pie finishes baking, sprinkle over the pumpkin. Then return the pie to the oven for the remaining baking time to glaze.

STRAWBERRY CUSTARD PIE

3 eggs, slightly beaten	Unbaked 9-inch pie shell
6 tablespoons sugar	1 quart strawberries
1/4 teaspoon salt	1 cup sugar
3 cups milk	1⅓ cups water
1 teaspoon vanilla	3 tablespoons cornstarch

Set oven for hot, 425°F. Combine eggs, sugar, and salt. Add milk slowly; stir in vanilla. Pour into pie shell. Bake 40 minutes, or till knife inserted near rim comes out clean. Chill.

Wash strawberries; hull. Simmer 1 cup of the berries, sugar, and 1 cup of the water 15 minutes. Mix remaining water with cornstarch; add to cooked berries. Cook until thick, stirring constantly; cool. Add uncooked berries. Spoon over pie. Chill. Makes 1 pie.

CHERRY PIE (inside front cover): Set oven for hot, 400°F. Prepare **1 recipe for pastry.** Roll out half the pastry 1/8 inch thick. Line 9-inch pie pan; trim 1/4 inch from edge. Combine **3½ cups pitted, fresh sour red cherries, 1¼ cups sugar,** and **1/4 cup flour.** Pour into pie shell. Dot with **1 tablespoon butter or margarine.** Roll out remaining pastry; cut in 1/2-inch strips. Arrange, lattice-fashion, over fruit. Seal edges; trim and flute. Bake 40 to 45 minutes. Makes 1 pie.

BUTTERSCOTCH BANANA PIE

2 cups milk	3 egg yolks, slightly beaten
3/4 cup brown sugar, firmly packed	2 tablespoons butter or margarine
1/3 cup flour	1/2 teaspoon vanilla
1/2 teaspoon salt	Baked 9-inch pie shell
	3 ripe bananas

Sweetened whipped cream

Heat milk in top of double boiler. Combine sugar, flour, and salt. Stir slowly into milk, mixing thoroughly. Cook over rapidly boiling water until thickened, stirring constantly. Cook 10 minutes longer, stirring occasionally. Stir a small amount of the hot mixture into egg yolks; then pour back into remaining hot mixture while beating vigorously. Cook 1 minute longer. Remove from heat. Add butter and vanilla. Cool thoroughly. Cover bottom of pie shell with small amount of filling. Peel bananas. Arrange alternate layers of sliced bananas and filling in pie shell, using filling for top layer. Top with sweetened whipped cream and additional banana slices, if desired. Makes 1 pie.

BANANA CREAM PIE: Prepare filling from **packaged vanilla pudding mix** or filling for Coconut Cream Pie (see p. 101). Pour into **baked pie shell** with **bananas** as directed above.

OLD-FASHIONED APPLE PIE

Recipe pastry
6 to 8 tart apples, pared
    and sliced
1 cup sugar

2 teaspoons flour
Dash nutmeg
1/2 teaspoon cinnamon
2 tablespoons butter or margerine

Set oven for hot, 400°F. Roll out half the pastry 1/8 inch thick. Line a 9-inch pie pan and trim 1/4 inch from rim. Arrange apples in shell. Mix sugar, flour, and spices; sprinkle over apples. Dot with butter. Roll out remaining pastry 1/8 inch thick. Cut slit for steam to escape. Adjust pastry over apples and trim 1/2 inch from rim of pan. Fold edge of top pastry under edge of lower pastry. Press edges together and flute or crimp. Bake 45 minutes or until apples are tender. Makes 1 pie.

DEEP DISH APPLE PIE: Set oven for hot, 400°F. Pare and core **6 tart apples.** Cut in eighths. Place in a 9-inch square greased baking dish. Combine **1/2 cup sugar, 1/2 cup brown sugar,** firmly packed, **dash nutmeg, dash cloves, grated rind of 1 lemon,** and **grated rind of 1 orange.** Mix well and sprinkle over apples. Dot with **3 tablespoons butter or margarine.** Roll out **1/2 recipe pastry.** Adjust over apples. Prick with a fork. Bake 45 minutes or till apples are tender. Makes 6 servings.

PEACH PARFAIT PIE

1¼ cups water or fruit juice
1 package raspberry gelatin
1 pint peach ice cream

1 cup chopped, sweetened
   fresh peaches
Baked 9-inch pie shell

Heat water to boiling in a 2-quart saucepan. Remove from heat. **Add** gelatin. Stir till dissolved. Add ice cream by spoonfuls, stirring **until** melted. Chill until mixture is thickened but not set, 15 to 20 minutes. Fold in peaches. Turn into pie shell; chill until firm, 30 to 35 minutes. Garnish with whipped cream and peach slices, if desired. Makes 1 pie. **Note:** If desired, use a **12-ounce package frozen peaches,** thawed and drained. Measure the juice; add **water** to make 1¼ cups liquid. **Vanilla ice cream** may be used in place of peach.

PASTRY (made with shortening): Sift together **2 cups sifted flour** and **1 teaspoon salt.** Cut in **1/3 cup shortening,** using 2 knives or a pastry blender, until mixture resembles coarse corn meal. Cut in another **1/3 cup shortening** until particles are size of small peas. Sprinkle **5 to 6 tablespoons water** over mixture, mixing with a fork until dough is moist enough to hold together. Press into a ball; chill well before rolling. Roll out on a lightly floured board or pastry cloth. Makes enough for one 8- or 9-inch 2-crust pie or two 8- or 9-inch 1-crust pies.

COCONUT CREAM PIE

2/3 cup sugar
1/2 cup flour
1/4 teaspoon salt
3 egg yolks, slightly beaten
2 cups milk

1 teaspoon vanilla
Baked 9-inch pie shell
1 cup whipping cream, whipped
   and sweetened to taste
Toasted shredded coconut

Mix sugar, flour, and salt in top of a double boiler. Combine egg yolks and milk. Stir into flour mixture; blend well. Cook over hot water until thickened, stirring constantly. Cover; cook 10 minutes longer. Cool slightly; add vanilla. Pour into pie shell. Cool. Just before serving, spread cream over filling and top with coconut. Makes 1 pie.

TO TOAST COCONUT: Spread shredded moist-pack coconut in a thin layer on a baking sheet. Place in broiler 3 to 4 inches below heat, 3 to 5 minutes. Watch carefully and stir with a fork.

CUSTARD PIE: Beat **3 eggs** slightly. Stir in **1/2 cup sugar** and 1/4 **teaspoon salt.** Gradually add **3 cups hot milk**; mix well. Stir in **1 teaspoon vanilla.** Pour into **unbaked 9-inch pie shell.** Sprinkle with **nutmeg.** Bake in hot oven, 425°F., 40 minutes, or until a knife inserted near rim comes out clean.

BLUEBERRY PIE

1 quart fresh blueberries	1 cup sugar
Recipe pastry	2 tablespoons flour
1 teaspoon vinegar	Nutmeg
2 tablespoons butter or margarine	

Set oven for hot, 425°F. Wash and pick over blueberries. Roll out half the pastry 1/8 inch thick. Line a 9-inch pie pan and trim 1/4 inch from rim. Pour berries into pastry shell. Combine vinegar, sugar, flour, and nutmeg; sprinkle over berries. Dot with butter. Roll out remaining pastry. Cut slit for steam to escape. Adjust over berries and trim 1/2 inch from rim of pan. Fold edge of top pastry under edge of lower pastry. Press edges together and flute or crimp. Or, cut pastry for top in long strips about 3/4 inch wide and arrange over berries in circles, as shown below. Bake 10 minutes. Reduce heat to moderately hot, 375°F.; bake 25 minutes longer, or until brown. Makes 1 pie. Note: You can use frozen blueberries in place of fresh. Two 12-ounce boxes make a 9-inch pie. Decrease sugar to 1/2 cup.

LEMON BLUEBERRY PIE: Pour berries into pastry shell. Arrange **very thin slices of lemon** over top. Sprinkle with sugar mixture; dot with butter. Cover with pastry; bake as directed.

PECAN PIE

1/2 cup butter or margarine	1/4 teaspoon salt
1 cup sugar	1 teaspoon vanilla
3 eggs, slightly beaten	1½ cups chopped pecans
3/4 cup dark corn syrup	Unbaked 9-inch pie shell

Whole pecan meats

Set oven for moderately hot, 375°F.

Cream butter. Add sugar gradually and continue beating until light and fluffy. Add next 5 ingredients and mix well. Pour into pie shell. Bake 40 to 45 minutes. Decorate edge of pie with whole pecans. Serve with whipped cream, if desired. Makes 1 pie.

CHOCOLATE BROWNIE PIE

Set oven for moderately hot, 375°F. Combine **3 well-beaten eggs, 1/2 cup sugar, 2 squares unsweetened chocolate,** melted, **2 tablespoons melted butter, 3/4 cup dark corn syrup.** Beat thoroughly with a rotary beater. Stir in **3/4 cup broken walnuts.** Pour into **unbaked 9-inch pie shell.** Bake 40 to 50 minutes or, until set. Serve, slightly warm or cold. Makes 1 pie.

ORANGE CHIFFON PIE

1 tablespoon unflavored gelatine	1/4 teaspoon salt
1/4 cup cold water	3/4 cup sugar
4 eggs, separated	Baked 9-inch pie shell
2 tablespoons lemon juice	1½ tablespoons grated orange rind
1/2 cup orange juice	Sweetened whipped cream

Soften gelatine in cold water. Beat egg yolks until light. Stir in lemon juice, orange juice, salt, and 1/2 cup of the sugar. Cook over hot, not boiling, water till thickened; stir constantly. Add gelatine; stir till dissolved. Chill until mixture begins to thicken. Whip egg whites till stiff; gradually beat in remaining sugar and orange rind. Fold into gelatine mixture. Pile in pastry shell. Chill until firm. Top with whipped cream and additional grated orange rind, if desired. Makes 1 pie.

PASTRY (made with oil): Sift together **2 cups sifted flour** and **1 teaspoon salt**. Combine **1/2 cup salad or cooking oil** and **5 tablespoons ice water**. Beat with a fork till thickened and creamy. Pour immediately (all at once) over the surface of the flour. Toss and mix with a fork. Form into a ball. Roll between 2 squares of waxed paper or on an unfloured board. Makes enough for one 8- or 9-inch 2-crust pie or two 8- or 9-inch 1-crust pies.

The Cookie Jar

Is there a cookie jar in your kitchen? Or, in the rush of everyday living, have you forgotten what fun it is to have cookies (of your own making) ready to serve to an unexpected caller, for the kids and their friends, or to have as a bedtime snack, with a glass of cool milk and a tart, red apple?

Drop cookies, cookie cut-outs in amusing shapes, fancy cookies made with a modern, easy-to-use press, pinwheels, squares and bars, macaroons, kisses—there is no limit to the variety of these home-made goodies.

Use confectioners' sugar instead of flour on the pastry board, rolling pin and cookie cutter when you are making cut-out cookies. It will disappear during the baking, improve flavor, and add crispness. And have you seen the 3-D plastic cutters? These are made in shapes for all the holidays and special occasions and the deep outlines make it easy to follow the design in frosting and ornamenting the cookies. A rich cookie dough of the shortbread variety is best for use with 3-D cutters, because it will not spread or lose its shape during baking.

Follow the recipes that come with a cookie press for best results. You will be amazed and delighted with the professional-looking fancy cookies that you can make so easily with one of these presses.

Certain types of cookies, like brownies, bar-cookies and some drop cookies make good travellers. A clean three-pound shortening container filled with cookies and packed in a box will travel well and keep the cookies fresh. Use transparent tape to secure the cover. The container will serve as a cookie jar until the cookies are gone—a fact that will be appreciated by the boys in service, or boys and girls in schools and colleges. As an added touch of thoughtfulness, strip the original paper label from the can and apply gay decals to make it attractive enough to keep on display, and in use!

Our Molasses Walnut and Banana Oatmeal Cookies will prove the salvation of the mothers whose pre-school toddlers are constantly begging for something to eat. These simple cookies will satisfy their hunger without spoiling appetites for meals to follow. Frosted, they are your answer to "What's for dessert?"

For children's parties, delight young guests by writing their names on the cookies with Confectioners' Sugar Icing (page 77).

So dust off your own cookie jar, light the oven, and bake a batch of cookies. Once you see what fun it can be, you'll make it a once-a-week habit from then on. Begin with one of the recipes that follow—then try them all!

MOLASSES WALNUT COOKIES

3/4 cup shortening	2 eggs, well-beaten
1 cup brown sugar, firmly packed	3½ cups sifted flour
1/2 cup molasses	1/2 teaspoon salt
3 tablespoons water	1 teaspoon baking soda
	1/2 cup chopped walnuts

Set oven for hot, 400°F. Cream shortening; add brown sugar; cream thoroughly. Add molasses and water. Add eggs; mix thoroughly. Sift together flour, salt, and baking soda; add with nuts to egg mixture; mix well. Drop by tablespoonfuls on a greased baking sheet. Bake 10 to 12 minutes. Cool on a rack. Makes 5 dozen.

SCOTCH SHORTBREAD: Cream **1 cup butter or margarine.** Add **3/4 cup confectioners' sugar** slowly. Add **1/2 teaspoon vanilla, dash of salt.** Stir in **2 cups sifted flour;** work smooth. Roll out 1/2 inch thick; cut with fluted cutter. Bake in moderate oven, 350°F., 25 minutes. Makes about 2 dozen cookies.

COCONUT JUMBLES: Prepare **cookie mix** as directed on package for rolled cookies. Roll out 1/8 inch thick; cut with doughnut cutter. Brush tops with **slightly beaten egg white;** sprinkle with **shredded coconut.** Bake in hot oven, 400°F., 8 minutes or till brown.

BANANA OATMEAL COOKIES

1½ cups sifted flour	3/4 cup shortening
1 cup sugar	1 egg, well-beaten
1/2 teaspoon baking soda	1 cup mashed ripe bananas
1 teaspoon salt	(2 to 3 bananas)
3/4 teaspoon cinnamon	1/2 cup chopped nuts
1/4 teaspoon nutmeg	1¾ cups rolled oats

Set oven for hot, 400°F.

Sift together first 6 ingredients into a large mixing bowl. Cut in shortening. Add egg, mashed bananas, nuts, and rolled oats. Beat until thoroughly mixed. Drop by teaspoonfuls, about 1½ inches apart, on an ungreased baking sheet. Top with whole walnut meats, if desired. Bake 12 to 15 minutes or until light brown. Remove immediately from pan; cool on a rack. Makes 3½ dozen.

DROP COOKIES: Cream **1¼ cups shortening** and **1 cup sugar** until fluffy. Add **3 eggs,** one at a time, beating well after each addition. Add **1 teaspoon vanilla.** Sift together **3¼ cups sifted flour** and **1/2 teaspoon salt;** add gradually to egg mixture; stir till smooth. Drop by teaspoonfuls on greased baking sheets; flatten with back of spoon or tines of fork pressed to form a cross. Bake in hot oven, 400°F., 10 minutes. Makes about 5 dozen cookies.

PEANUT BUTTER COOKIES

1/4 cup shortening	1½ cups flour
1 cup sugar	1/4 teaspoon salt
1/2 cup peanut butter	1/2 teaspoon baking soda
2 eggs, well-beaten	1 teaspoon cinnamon
1/4 cup milk	3/4 cup seedless raisins
1 teaspoon vanilla	3/4 cup rolled oats

Set oven for moderate, 350°F. Cream shortening; add sugar; cream thoroughly. Add peanut butter; mix well. Stir in eggs, milk, and vanilla. Sift together flour, salt, baking soda, and cinnamon; stir into egg mixture. Fold in raisins and rolled oats. Drop by teaspoonfuls, about 2 inches apart, on an ungreased baking sheet. Bake 15 minutes or until brown. Makes about 3½ dozen.

CHEESE PINWHEEL COOKIES: Blend **two 3-ounce packages cream cheese** and **1 cup butter or margarine;** cut into **2 cups sifted flour** with 2 knives or pastry blender. Knead into soft ball. Wrap in waxed paper. Chill well. Roll out 1/8 inch thick in oblong. Spread with **1/2 cup softened tart jelly,** sprinkle with **1/2 cup finely chopped walnuts.** Roll up like jelly roll. Cut crosswise in thin slices. Bake on greased baking sheet in hot oven, 400°F., 15 minutes, or until delicate brown. Makes about 3 dozen.

BROWNIES

1/2 cup butter or margarine	1 teaspoon vanilla
2 squares unsweetened chocolate	1 cup sifted cake flour
	1/4 teaspoon baking powder
2 eggs	1/4 teaspoon salt
1 cup sugar	1 cup chopped walnuts

Set oven for moderate, 350°F. Grease an 8-inch square pan.

Melt butter and chocolate together over hot water. Beat eggs; add sugar gradually while beating. Add chocolate mixture to egg mixture. Add vanilla; beat hard 1 minute. Sift together flour, baking powder, and salt. Stir into chocolate mixture. Add nuts; mix well. Pour into the pan. Bake 35 to 40 minutes, or until browned. Cut into squares or strips. Makes about 16 brownies.

FUDGE BARS: Bake Brownies (above); cool in the pan without cutting. Melt **2 squares unsweetened chocolate** over hot water; combine **1/4 cup sugar** and **3 tablespoons water**; stir over medium heat until sugar dissolves; boil 1 minute. Pour slowly into the melted chocolate, stirring constantly. Beat until thick. Add **1/2 teaspoon vanilla**. Spread on Brownies. When set, cut in bars 4 inches long and 1 inch wide. Makes 16 Fudge Bars.

FRUIT BARS

3/4 cup sifted flour	1/4 cup melted shortening
1/2 teaspoon baking powder	2 eggs, well-beaten
1/2 teaspoon salt	1 cup chopped nuts
1 cup brown sugar,	1 cup chopped pitted
firmly packed	dates

Set oven for moderate, 350°F. Grease a 9-inch square pan.

Sift together flour, baking powder, and salt; add sugar; mix well. Combine shortening and eggs; stir into dry ingredients and blend well. Stir in nuts and dates. Turn into greased pan and bake 30 minutes or till browned. Cut into bars while hot. Makes about 16 bars.

MINCEMEAT SQUARES: Set oven for hot, 400°F. Grease a 9-inch square pan. Combine **1 cup firmly packed brown sugar, 1¼ cups rolled oats, 1½ cups sifted flour,** and **1/2 teaspoon salt;** mix well. Cut in **3/4 cup shortening** with 2 knives or pastry blender until it has consistency of coarse crumbs. Spread half the mixture in the greased pan; combine **2 cups mincemeat** and **1/2 teaspoon each lemon and orange flavoring;** spread over first mixture in pan; top with remaining flour mixture. Bake 20 to 25 minutes. Cool slightly and cut in squares. Makes about 16 squares.

The Delight of Desserts

What can be said—what needs to be said—about desserts? The menu builds up to a climax—looks forward to a perfect ending—dessert. The diner's delight—the dieter's despair! The reward for good children, the appeaser of mankind's sweet tooth.

If your family loves desserts they will never be able to resist our Cheese Cake with Strawberry Glaze (the best cheese cake, we swear, with or without the glaze, that ever came out of an oven), our ruby and gold Peach Cobbler, or our brilliant and beautiful Cranberry Banana Betty. Perhaps one word of advice, serve a light dessert after a heavy meal, a rich dessert to top off a less-satisfying one.

And on the days when a long afternoon's shopping, or the baby's fussing, or heavy housework calls for a hurriedly-prepared dinner, don't forget the wonderful variety of packaged pudding mixes that are available. Made in jig time, these are delicious served plain or with cream, or combined with fruit, fresh, frozen, or canned. They're excellent for the small fry too, especially for those too young to have the sweeter desserts we grown-ups love.

And of course for a richer ready-to-eat dessert, there are available canned, steamed plum, date, and fig puddings.

We think whipped cream on dessert is just like frosting on cake, and accordingly want variety. So we're giving you our suggestions to add extra zest to your desserts.

1. **Spiced Whipped Cream:** For each cup of whipping cream, use about 1/4 teaspoon cinnamon, nutmeg, or cloves. Add to the cream with the sugar. Or a dash of each makes a pleasing combination.

2. **Coffee Whipped Cream:** Add about a teaspoon of instant coffee powder to the cream with the sugar.

3. **Chocolate-flavored Whipped Cream:** Add 1 teaspoon of cocoa to the cream with the sugar.

4. For sweetening whipped cream, try brown sugar instead of confectioners'. It's especially good combined with spices or instant coffee powder.

The mother whose kiddies just won't drink their milk will especially welcome the bread puddings (page 116), a wonderfully subtle way to add to the family's milk diet. Fruits are excellent nutritional foods too. A cake or cookie dessert becomes more important and satisfying served with a dish of fruit.

Whether it be dessert for a bridge luncheon, the finishing touch to a company dinner, or just the family meal, we know any one of the recipes that follow will make a memorable event of the occasion!

CHEESE CAKE WITH STRAWBERRY GLAZE

1/2 cup butter, softened	3 tablespoons flour
1 package zweiback, crushed	1½ teaspoons grated orange rind
1/2 cup very fine sugar	1/2 teaspoon vanilla
1 tablespoon grated lemon rind	5 eggs, unbeaten
2½ pounds cream cheese	2 egg yolks
1¾ cups granulated sugar	1/4 cup whipping cream

Set oven for very low, 250°F. Grease bottom and sides of 9-inch spring-form pan. Combine first 3 ingredients and 1/2 tablespoon grated lemon rind. Press on bottom and sides of pan, reserving about 1/3 cup. Combine next 5 ingredients and remaining lemon rind; beat until smooth and fluffy. Add eggs and yolks one at a time stirring in lightly. Stir in cream. Spoon into pan over crumbs, spreading evenly. Sprinkle with remaining crumb mixture. Bake 1 hour. Turn off heat; leave in oven 1 hour. Remove from oven. Cool slowly to room temperature then chill. Remove from pan. Cover with **Strawberry Glaze.**

STRAWBERRY GLAZE: Combine **1 cup washed and hulled straw-berries, 1 cup water,** and **1 cup sugar** in saucepan; bring to a boil; simmer 15 minutes. Blend **3 tablespoons cornstarch** and **1/3 cup water.** Stir into sugar mixture. Cook; stir until thickened. Strain; cool. Arrange **whole berries** around edge of cheesecake. Pour glaze over berries, being sure each one is well coated.

GLAZED BAKED APPLES

4 large baking apples	**1 teaspoon cinnamon**
1/2 cup seedless	**2 teaspoons butter or margarine**
raisins	**2/3 cup boiling water**
2 tablespoons sugar	**1/2 cup sugar**
1 tablespoon grated lemon rind	**1/2 cup red currant jelly**

Wash and core apples; pare 1/3 the way down from stem. Place in a baking dish. Combine next 4 ingredients. Fill centers of apples. Top each with 1/2 teaspoon butter. Combine water and the 1/2 cup sugar; pour over apples. Boke uncovered, in moderate oven 350°F., 45 to 60 minutes, or till tender, basting often with syrup in bottom of pan. Remove from oven.

Melt jelly over low heat; stir with a fork. Spoon over apples. Place in broiler 3 inches from heat; broil 3 to 4 minutes, or till glazed. Serve warm or cold with cream. Makes 4 servings.

BAKED WINTER PEARS: Select **large pears** of uniform size; halve, core and peel. Fill centers with mixture of **brown sugar, raisins** and **chopped walnuts.** Place in baking dish with just enough water to cover bottom of dish. Sprinkle with a little more **sugar** mixed with **cinnamon.** Cover; bake in moderate oven, 350°F., 45 minutes or until tender. Serve with **sweetened whipped cream.**

CRANBERRY BANANA BETTY

1 cup brown sugar, firmly
    packed
3 cups soft bread crumbs
1/2 teaspoon cinnamon
1/4 teaspoon nutmeg

4 to 5 bananas
1 can cranberry sauce
1 lemon, juice and grated
    rind
2 tablespoons butter or margarine

Set oven for moderately hot, 375°F. Combine sugar, crumbs, and spices; reserve 1/2 cup. Peel and slice bananas; sprinkle with lemon juice. Arrange alternate layers of crumb mixture and bananas in a 1½-quart casserole. Spread cranberry sauce over top. Sprinkle reserved crumbs and lemon rind on top. Dot with butter. Bake 25 minutes. Serve warm or chilled with cream. Makes 6 servings.

FRUITED GELATIN WHIP (inside back cover): Prepare a **package cherry-flavored gelatin** with **water** as directed on package. Arrange a **few slices banana** in bottom of 1½-quart mold; add just enough gelatin mixture to "anchor" them. Chill till firm. Pour in more gelatin to fill mold 1/4 full. Chill till set. Chill remaining gelatin until thickened but not set; whip with rotary beater until fluffy; fold in **3/4 cup sliced bananas** and **1 cup pitted Bing cherries;** spoon over gelatin in mold. Chill till set. Unmold. Garnish with **additional fruit.** Serve with **whipped cream.** Makes 6 servings.

RAISIN RICE PUDDING

1/2 cup rice	3 eggs, beaten
1 quart milk	1 cup sugar
1/2 cup seedless raisins	1 teaspoon vanilla
1/3 cup butter or margarine	1/4 teaspoon salt
Cinnamon or nutmeg	

Combine rice with 2 cups of the milk in top of a double boiler; cook over hot water until rice is tender. Add raisins and butter. Combine eggs, sugar, vanilla, salt, and remaining milk. Stir into hot rice mixture. Pour into a greased 1½-quart baking dish. Sprinkle with cinnamon. Bake in moderate oven, 350°F., 20 to 30 minutes, or until set. Serve hot or cold. Makes 6 servings.

CREAMY RICE PUDDING: Scald **1 quart milk**; add **1/4 cup rice, 1/2 cup sugar, few grains salt,** and **3 tablespoons butter or margarine**; stir until sugar dissolves. Beat **3 eggs** slightly; pour milk mixture slowly on eggs. Pour in greased 1½-quart casserole; sprinkle with **nutmeg.** Set in pan of warm water; bake in moderately low oven, 325°F., 1¼ hours. Makes 6 servings.

SPICY RICE PUDDING: In either recipe above, add **1 large stick cinnamon** and **6 whole cloves** to milk; cook over hot water 30 minutes. Strain; proceed according to recipe.

QUEEN OF BREAD PUDDINGS

1 quart milk	3 tablespoons melted butter or
3 cups stale bread cubes	margarine
1 cup sugar	1/2 teaspoon vanilla
1/4 teaspoon salt	1/2 cup tart jelly, any flavor
3 egg yolks, beaten	3 egg whites

Scald milk. Pour over bread cubes. Add 1/2 cup of the sugar and salt. Add egg yolks, butter, and vanilla; mix well. Pour into a 1½-quart greased casserole. Set casserole in a baking pan. Pour in hot water to depth of 1 inch. Bake in moderate oven, 325°F., 45 minutes, or until set. Spread jelly over top. Whip egg whites stiff; fold in remaining 1/2 cup sugar gradually; swirl on jelly. Bake 20 minutes longer, or till brown; chill. Makes 6 to 8 servings.

CUSTARD BREAD PUDDING: Use **2 cups soft bread crumbs, 1/2 cup sugar** and **2 whole eggs** instead of quantities given in above recipe. Omit jelly and meringue.

MYSTERY PUDDING: Use plain **whole wheat** or **raisin-whole wheat bread** instead of white bread in making Custard Bread Pudding.

CHOCOLATE BREAD PUDDING: Add **2 squares unsweetened chocolate,** melted, to bread and milk mixture in Custard Bread Pudding.

RASPBERRY TAPIOCA PARFAIT

1 egg white	1/4 teaspoon nutmeg
5 tablespoons sugar	1/8 teaspoon vanilla
1 egg yolk	2 teaspoons lemon juice
2 cups milk	1 teaspoon grated lemon rind
3 tablespoons quick- cooking tapioca	1 cup whipping cream, whipped
	1 cup quick-frozen raspberries
1/2 teaspoon salt	or sweetened, fresh raspberries

Whip egg white until foamy. Add 2 tablespoons of the sugar, 1 tablespoon at a time; continue beating until mixture stands in very soft peaks. Set aside. Mix egg yolk with a small amount of the milk in saucepan. Add remaining milk, tapioca, remaining 3 tablespoons sugar, salt, and nutmeg. Place over medium heat; cook until mixture comes to a boil, stirring constantly. Pour small amount of hot mixture into beaten egg white; blend. Add remaining mixture gradually, stirring constantly. Add vanilla, lemon juice, and rind. Cool; stir after 15 or 20 minutes. Fold into whipped cream. Fill parfait glasses with alternate layers of pudding and raspberries. Top with additional berries and whipped cream, if desired. Makes 8 servings.

STRAWBERRY TAPIOCA PARFAIT: Use **frozen or sweetened fresh strawberries** in place of the raspberries.

PEACH COBBLER

1 cup sugar	1 cup water
2 tablespoons cornstarch	2 tablespoons butter or margarine
1/2 teaspoon cinnamon	5 cups sliced, pared fresh peaches

BISCUIT TOPPING

1½ cups biscuit mix	2/3 cup light cream
4 tablespoons sugar	2 teaspoons grated orange rind

Set oven for very hot, 450°F. Blend the 1 cup sugar, cornstarch, and cinnamon in large saucepan; add water. Bring to boiling, stirring constantly. Remove from heat. Add butter and peaches. Pour into a shallow baking dish. Combine biscuit mix and 2 tablespoons sugar; blend in cream with a fork. Drop dough in 6 mounds around edge of baking dish. Combine 2 remaining tablespoons sugar and orange rind; sprinkle on dough. Bake 25 minutes, or until peaches are tender and biscuits golden brown. Serve warm with plain or whipped cream. Makes 6 generous servings.

COBBLER VARIATIONS: There are many other fruits which make wonderful cobblers: Sliced pared tart apples, sliced pared pears (with a little lemon juice added), pitted sweet or sour cherries, blueberries, pitted apricots, raspberries or strawberries.

Tricks with Leftovers

Every thrifty housewife is eager to make the money spent on food stretch as far as possible. This, of course, means wise use of leftovers. With a little imagination, these foods make a dish, so good, your family will think you have planned it that way. Here are some recipes you will find in the book for using leftovers, and some additional money-saving suggestions.

MEATS AND POULTRY

Meat from the Sunday roast provides a wonderful beginning for Shepherd's Pie (page 32). Use meat left from baked ham in Chef's Salad (page 63); leftover chicken or turkey can be used for Chicken Tetrazzini (page 41) and Hawaiian Turkey Curry (page 44). Creamed chicken, turkey, or ham served with waffles (page 82) makes a hearty luncheon or supper dish.

Try some of these ideas for variety:

LITTLE MEAT PIES: Moisten **ground or finely chopped cooked meat—** any kind—with **gravy or condensed tomato or cream of mushroom soup.** Roll out **pastry** and cut in 4-inch squares. Put meat mixture in center. Fold over diagonally; seal edges. Bake in hot oven, 400°F., 15 to 20 minutes, or till brown. Perfect for lunch box toters.

BAKED MEAT PUFF: Combine equal parts **chopped cooked meat** (any kind, but ham is especially good) and **chopped Swiss cheese.** Add a little **grated onion.** Spread thickly between slices of **white bread,** sandwich-fashion. Arrange sandwiches in a single layer in a well-greased baking dish. For 4 sandwiches, combine **4 beaten eggs, 2 cups milk,** and **1/2 teaspoon salt.** Pour over sandwiches. Let stand 1 hour. Bake in hot oven, 400°F., 40 minutes, or until puffy and golden brown. Fine for luncheon or Sunday night supper.

MEAT 'N' CHEESE SANDWICH BROIL: Chop any kind of **cooked meat;** season with **grated onion, salt, and pepper;** moisten with **ketchup, mayonnaise, or salad dressing.** Toast bread on one side. Spread untoasted sides with meat mixture; top with a slice of **processed American cheese;** broil till bubbly and brown.

MEAT SCRAMBLE: Stir **finely chopped cooked meat** into **scrambled egg mixture;** cook as usual. Good in omelet, too.

STUFFED EGGS: Season **mashed cooked egg yolk mixture** with **minced meat**—ham, pork, chicken, or tongue; refill the **egg white halves.**

VEGETABLES

Mashed potatoes lose their appeal when warmed over as such but they become something special in French Fried Potato Puffs (page 13) or as the topping on Shepherd's Pie (page 32).

Peas, green beans, and lima beans are fine in Shepherd's Pie, or stir them into Beef Stew or Lamb Stew just before serving and heat well. Try them for making Cream of Vegetable Soup (page 8) or Vegetable Salad Medley (page 69), or add them to a tossed green salad.

Broccoli and spinach make delicious Cream of Vegetable Soup. That leftover cup of corn is fine for Corn Griddle Cakes (page 83).

Save the fresh green leaves from celery. Shredded, they add flavor to a tossed salad, and to stews and soups.

Tops from green onions make delicious topping to sprinkle over cream soups in place of chives and are good in green salads.

When a recipe calls for a little grated onion or a few drops of onion juice, save what is left of the onion. Wrap it in waxed paper or aluminum foil; store in the refrigerator for later use.

OTHER IDEAS

Grate small pieces of cheese and store in a tightly covered jar in refrigerator. Sprinkle over casserole dishes of vegetables and meats. (See Baked Meat Puff, page 119.) They perk up a cream sauce for vegetables, too.

Bread which has lost its freshness is ideal for Queen of Bread Puddings (page 116) or for Cranberry Banana Betty (page 114). To make bread crumbs for future use, put bread in a very low oven to dry thoroughly. Then roll till crumbs are fine. Store in a tightly covered jar to use for such dishes as Breaded Veal Cutlet (page 22), Fried Fish Fillets (page 46), or for topping on a casserole or oven dish such as Deviled Crabmeat (page 53).

Bacon fat, strained of course, gives added flavor to molasses and spice cookies and you can use chicken fat in the same way. Chicken fat is excellent for frying chicken or for making a cream sauce for creamed chicken dishes.

Grate the peel of breakfast oranges and mix with granulated sugar, about a tablespoon to a half cup. Store in a tightly covered jar to sprinkle over biscuits, rolls, or cookies before baking.

Menus

LUNCHEONS

LUNCHEON 1
Consommé Madrilène
Tuna Filled Cheese-Noodle Ring*
French Bread
Cucumber and Water Cress Salad
Raspberry Tapioca Parfait*
Coffee or Tea

LUNCHEON 2
Creme Vichysoisse*
Chef's Salad*
French Bread
Peach Cobbler*   Coffee or Tea

LUNCHEON 3
Chicken Consommé
Assorted Cold Cuts
Golden Potato Salad*
Sliced Tomatoes   Hard Rolls
Peach Parfait Pie*
Coffee or Tea

LUNCHEON 4
Cold Borscht
Deviled Crabmeat*
Tossed Raw Vegetable Salad
Hot Baking Powder Biscuits*
Sliced Peaches   Tea

LUNCHEON 5
Salmon Salad Bowl*
Blue Cheese Dressing*
Salt Sticks
Strawberry Ice Cream
Brownies*   Hot Coffee or Tea

SPECIAL OCCASIONS

EASTER BRUNCH
Chilled Fruit Juice
Broiled Ham Slice
Hot Cross Buns*   Scrambled Eggs
Apricot Preserves
Strawberry Jam
Coffee

FOURTH OF JULY DINNER
Broiled Salmon Steaks*
Cucumber Sauce*
Buttered Zucchini
Mashed Potatoes
Poppy Seed Rolls   Relishes
Cherry Pie*   Iced Coffee

THANKSGIVING DINNER
Cream of Oyster Soup*
Roast Turkey*
Mushroom Stuffing*
Giblet Gravy
Candied Sweet Potatoes
Buttered Broccoli
Celery   Cranberry Sauce   Olives
Pumpkin Pie*   Coffee

CHRISTMAS DINNER
Cranberry Juice Cocktail
Roast Pork*
Green Beans   Whipped Potatoes
Hubbard Squash
Celery   Olives   Pickles
Pecan Pie*   Coffee

*See index for recipe page number.

Menus

SPRING and SUMMER

DINNER 1

Roast Chicken*
Asparagus Hollandaise
Scalloped Corn
Tomato Aspic Salad
Blueberry Pie*   Coffee or Tea

DINNER 2

Shrimp Jambalaya*
Fried Bananas
Tossed Green Salad
Coffee Ice Cream
Coconut Jumbles*   Tea

DINNER 3

Roast Leg of Lamb*
Creamed New Potatoes with Chives
Mint Jelly   Buttered Carrots
Water Cress Salad
Cheese Cake—Strawberry Glaze*
Coffee or Tea

DINNER 4

Shish Kebab*
Assorted Relishes
Tossed Salad   French Bread
Strawberry Shortcake
Coffee or Tea

DINNER 5

Baked Stuffed Sea Bass*
Lobster Sauce*
Green Peas   Relishes
Hard Rolls
Lord Baltimore Cake*
Coffee

FALL and WINTER

DINNER 1

Appetizer Salad
Standing Rib Roast of Beef*
French Fried Potato Puffs*
Harvard Beets   Green Peas
Old-Fashioned Apple Pie*
Coffee   Cheese

DINNER 2

Chicken Fricassee*
Baking Powder Biscuits*   Gravy
Spinach   Baked Acorn Squash
Currant Jelly
Pecan Ice Cream   Fruit Bars*
Coffee or Tea

DINNER 3

Barbecued Spareribs with
Potatoes and Sauerkraut*
Buttered Green Beans
Fruited Gelatin Whip*
Coffee or Tea

DINNER 4

Italian Spaghetti*
Bread Sticks
Tossed Green Salad
Fresh Fruit
Assorted Cheese   Coffee

DINNER 5

London Broil—Mushroom Gravy*
Parslied Carrots
Buttered Limas
Hard Rolls   Tossed Salad
Banana Chiffon Cake*
Coffee or Tea

Index

Index

Index

Index

Index

BLUEBERRY MUFFINS
page 81